# SAMURAI
# LEADERS

# SAMURAI LEADERS

## FROM THE TENTH TO THE NINETEENTH CENTURY

MICHAEL SHARPE

METRO BOOKS
NEW YORK

This 2008 edition published by
Metro Books, by arrangement with
Compendium Publishing Ltd.

Designer: Danny Gillespie
Color Reproduction:
Anorax Imaging Ltd

Metro Books
122 Fifth Avenue
New York, NY 10011

ISBN-13: 978-1-4351-0399-3
ISBN-10: 1-4351-0399-8

Printed and bound in China

1  3  5  7  9  10  8  6  4  2

**Acknowledgments**
Thanks to Clive Sinclaire and Jo St
Mart for photo research; to Margaret
Vaudry for the index; Danny
Gillespie for design.

# Contents

**Page 1:** Three 19th century Samurai. Man at left carries a *naginata* (halberd); man at right a straight spear (su-yari); bowman's sword has a bear fur scabbard cover. *via Clive Sinclaire*

**Previous pages:** Kimura Shigenari enjoyed the rank of *Nogato no kami*. He was defeated by Ii Naotaka and killed at the battle of Wakae on June 3, 1615. *via Clive Sinclaire*

**Left:** An image from the famous story of the 47 Ronin as they use a war mallet to break down the door to Kira Kozukenosuke Yoshinaka's mansion to kill him, December 14, 1702. *via Clive Sinclaire*

日本武尊

# Introduction

*Samurai Leaders* brings together the biographical details of more than 100 significant figures in the history of feudal Japan, at the time when the samurai class was pre-eminent in her society. Although by no means comprehensive, neither is this an arbitrary selection. The characters in this book were selected for their diversity, and the scope is wide. Here you will find heroes and villains, some strong and others weak, and among them, tragic, cunning, cultivated and memorable personalities whose lives in some way impacted on the events of their time. The power struggles between these men dominated Japanese history for hundreds of years.

Although most of them at some time served in a military capacity as samurai *tai shogun* (military commanders), some were leaders by merit of their power and influence in other quarters. One example is Minamoto Yoshitomo. Undoubtedly outclassed on the battlefield by many of his contemporaries, nevertheless his skill and shrewdness in the political sphere saw him elevated to a position of supreme authority as the first shogun of Japan. It would be unrepresentative, therefore, to limit ourselves strictly to men who lived and died as warriors. There were a great many of those, and important and influential characters are missing from this book. A truly definitive listing would be a mighty tome indeed, and someone will

**Left:** The story of Yamato Takeru is one of the earliest legends of Japan. He is seen bearing the fabled sword *Kusanagi no tsurugi* during a battle with a teacherous lord who set fire to grassland to kill him. *via Clive Sinclaire*

inevitably always be omitted. However, it is hoped that herein you will find much to inform and entertain, and inspire further research into Japan's long and fascinating history.

All of the men whose biographies appear in this book held some rank or title within the upper echelons of Japanese society. In theory, the position of supreme authority was that of the *tenno*, or emperor. During the Heian Period through the so-called *insei* system there were in fact two emperors, one sitting and the other cloistered. Some of these emperors, most notably Go-Shirakawa (1053–1129, r. 1073–1087 and cloistered rule 1087–1129), were extremely powerful. However, with a few exceptions, notably Go-Daigo (1288–1339), after the establishment of the Kamakura shogunate at the end of the twelfth century the emperor was a purely a figurehead, a leader in title only. True power lay behind the throne, and prior to about 1200, this was concentrated in the hands of just a small group of families, which had risen from the early days of the Japanese court to dominate the affairs of court and jealously guarded the status quo.

By tradition, these families filled the positions of the *kugyo*, a collective term for the tiny group of few men attached to the court of the Emperor. In general, this elite group included only three to four men at a time. The positions included that of *Sessho*, *Daijo-daijin*, (Chancellor of the Realm or Chief Minister) *Sadaijin* (Minister of the Left), *Udaijin* (Minister of the Right) *Nadaijin* (Minister of the Center) and *Dainagon* (Major Counsellor). There were many other positions, but as with the formal court, during

the Nara and Heian periods there was a marked decline in their power and influence, which reached a low point under the Tokugawa shogunate.

Also from among these families came the first men to be called shogun. In the eighth century the temporary position of *Seii Tai* shogun was that of a military commander in the service of the court; four centuries later the shogun had superseded the emperor as the true leader. Then, over time, the position of shogun itself began to lose its commanding authority when through a process of devolution,

**Left:** A spectacular 15th century helmet signed by maker Miochin Nobuiye. *via Clive Sinclaire*

**Right:** Full face armor dating from the 18th century signed by Miochin Yoshiyasu. It is missing a moustache. *via Clive Sinclaire*

subordinates in the provinces clambered up and eventually subsumed their former masters. Clans such as the Fujiwara, who enjoyed a position of unparalleled authority in the Heian court, were slowly transplanted by their strong-grown rural cousins. At the end of the lengthy *Sengoku jidai* (usually translated as the era of warring states), the supremacy of the shogun was temporarily re-established, but his authority (if not that of the shogunate itself) was progressively diminished.

During the Muromachi period and for most of the *Sengoku jidai*, there was the position of *shikken* (regent) under the shogun (or more accurately regents as after 1337 there were two). Their responsibilities and titles changed, but many exerted great influence over court decisions.

However, the greater number of the men herein described were what are called *daimyo*, or great names, who by merit of their land possessions, or *han*, and often more, were in a position of significant strength. The *daimyo* were an outgrowth of the *kokushi*, who from the eighth century were appointed by the Imperial Court in Kyoto to oversee a province, and by the shugo that supplanted them. The post of *shugo* (provincial governor) was an official position created in 1185 by the Kamakura shogunate to extend its rule over Japan. In theory, the *shugo* held not only military and police powers, but also economic power within a province. However, in practice, the ability of these men to effectively govern varied from one province to the next, dependent on the relative strength of local warlords (note for example, the cases of Abe no Yoritoki and Taira no Masakado).

When the *shugo* began to claim power over the lands they ostensibly supervised, we see the emergence in the late 15th century of the *daimyo*. Whereas in the Heian and Muromachi periods the major *shugo daimyo* were appointed from among the members a few well-connected clans, by the start of the Sengoku era many more clans had risen to prominence. Their *han* (domain) might comprise just a city (Oda Nobunaga in 1550), a clot of neighboring cities (Oda in 1558), a collection of scattered cities in several provinces (Takeda Shingen in 1540), several provinces (Oda and Takeda in 1575), an entire region (Tokugawa Ieyasu in 1590), or more than one region (Oda in 1582).

Traditionally, the title of *daimyo* was hereditary, passing from father to first-born son. But it was not always so simple. There are many instances where retainers flexed their political power to block the succession of an

**Below:** This image shows a moment from one of the most famous of all Japanese revenge stories, that of the Soga Brothers, often to be found in art and theater productions. Kawazu Sukeyasu, the father of the brothers—Juro Sukenari (1172–1193) and Goro Tokimune (1174–1193)—was killed in 1176 by Kudo Suketsune. The boys swore revenge, waiting many years until they were able to kill him, which they did when he was on a hunting trip on Mt. Fuji with Yoritomo. *via Clive Sinclaire*

**Below:** Eighteenth-century armor of the *domaru* style, with blue laces. *Domaru* armor passes round the torso and is tied at the side. The spectacular helmet is made from 62 individual plates. Note also the *mempo*—face armor—with its pronounced cheek protection, and *kutsu* (shoes) of bear fur. *via Clive Sinclaire*

unpopular sibling, and yet other examples of retainers rising from the ranks to wrest power from their erstwhile masters.

As we shall see, there was a great deal of conflict both within and between these men. The first catalyst was an innate hunger for power and influence, either within the family or at court. The whole of Japanese history is pock-marked with incidents of familial infighting, in which brother fought brother, father or uncle over some matter of succession, loyalty, honor or simple greed. Time and again we see examples of sons killing their fathers or siblings, and vice versa, or else sacrificed in the name of some greater good.

The other was land. *Daimyo* were entitled to certain privileges within their domains, the main one being the right to collect taxes (in the form of rice), and to raise troops. Initially, the court apportioned the rural fiefs, but by the Sengoku era this function had been assumed by certain of the most powerful *daimyo* who, dependent on the loyalty of their own retainer bands, were able to grant and confiscate territory at will. In turn *daimyo* commanded loyalty by gifting smaller parcels of land to their retainers and vassals, which effectively provided them with a source of income. As we shall see, the want of land emerged as a major cause of conflict.

But although conflict and warfare was an inexorable part of life over a period of hundreds of years, viewing the leaders of feudal Japan simply as ambitious, voracious and cruel warmongers is overly simplistic. In fact, if we look beyond the martial sphere, evidence of a much broader impact on the physical, social and political landscape of Japan can still be seen today. All of Japan's great castles were established in the Muromachi or Sengoku periods, as bastions of provincial power, and many great temples, houses and gardens were built through their patronage. The more refined patronised the arts, fostering among other things the Japanese theater (*kabuki*), the tea

ceremony, and provided the inspiration for much early Japanese literature. Furthermore, they created many of the political institutions that shaped the nation, her legal system, and fostered trading relations that brought new technologies to Japan and provided a market for her products. Finally, crucially, they made Japan militarily strong enough to resist Mongol invasions. Viewed as a whole that is an impressive legacy.

**Far right:** This armor has an embossed chest protector (*do*) and a 56-piece iron helmet signed by Minamoto Yoshikazu in 1851. He was a retainer of the *daimyo* of Ueda castle in Shinano. *via Clive Sinclaire*

**Right:** Unusual brick-red armor laced in blue, The helmet shape represented the cap of a Buddhist sect. The helmet is signed Nagasone Masanori who worked between 1673 and 1670 and the iron face armor by Miochin Muneyasu in the 19th century. *via Clive Sinclaire*

**Above:** Actors in the roles of Taira no Munemori, Mikazuki Osen, and Ebizako no Ju as painted by Utagawa Kuniyoshi (1798–1861), one of the last great masters of the Japanese *ukiyo-e* style of woodblock prints and painting. Taira no Munemori (1147–1185) was one of the Taira clan's main leaders during the Genpei War between the Taira and Minamoto clans in late-Heian period Japan.
*Library of Congress, Prints and Photographs Division, LC-DIG-jpd-00668*

**Glossary**

| | |
|---|---|
| bakufu | shogunate |
| betto | chief administrator |
| daijo daijin | chancellor |
| daimyo | feudal lord |
| do | chest protector |
| domaru | armor that wraps round torso and fastens at the side |
| Genpei kassen | wars of 1180–85 between Taira and Minamoto clans |
| Gosannen kassen | Later Three Years War—fighting in the 1080s in Mutsu province |
| go-tairo | council of five elders |
| han | domain |
| Heiji no ran | Heiji rebellion |
| Hogen no ran | Hogen rebellion |
| Ikko-ikki | Buddhist rebellions against lords during 15th and 16th centuries |
| insei system | Mainly seen in the 11th and 12th centuries, when a retired emperor exerted influence; also known as cloistered rule |
| jidai | age or period (eg Sengoku jidai) |
| kabuki | a form of Japanesetheater |
| kampaku | first secretary and regent who assists an adult emperor |
| kanrei | shogun's deputy |
| kokushi | provincal overlord |
| kutsu | shoes |
| mempo | face armor |
| naginata | halberd |
| o-kosho | teenage page |
| rensho | assistant to the regent |
| seii tai shogun | military commanders |
| Sengoku jidai | the Warring States period |
| Seppuku | ritual suicide by disembowelment |
| Sessho | regent to assist either a child emperor before coming of age or an empress |
| Shikken | regent for the shogun during the Kamakura shogunate |
| Shogun | general |
| Shugo | military governor |
| Sohei | warrior monks |
| tenno | emperor |
| Zenkunen gassen | Former Nine Years War |

# Abe no Yoritoki
## (d. 1057)
### Head of the Abe clan

Abe no Yoritoki was head of the Abe clan for a period during the eleventh century, best remembered as the catalyst of the *Zenkunen kassen* or Former Nine Years War. As the *chinjufu shogun* (general in charge of overseeing the *emishi*—northeastern Honshu—and the defense of the north), he was ruler of six *emishi* districts (Iwate, Hienuki, Shiwa, Isawa, Esashi and Waga) in Mutsu (modern day Iwate Prefecture). During his tenure over this remote domain Yoritoki became essentially autonomous, exceeding his authority by collecting taxes and confiscating property in defiance of the local Governor. In response the governor sent to Kyoto for help, which in turn provided the spark for the *Zenkunen* War. In 1051, Minamoto no Yoriyoshi and his son Yoshiie were sent to chastise Yoritoki, and restore power over the province to the governor. The Abe and Minamoto clans fought for nine years, with some truces, over the course of the next twelve years. In 1057, during the battle of the Koromogawa River, Yoritoki died from an arrow wound. His sons continued fighting for a time but were finally overwhelmed by the combined Minamoto and Kiyohara armies at Kuriyagawa in 1062.

# Abe no Sadato
## (1019–1062)
### Head of the Abe clan

Abe no Sadato was a Heian era samurai and head of the Abe clan. His father was the rebellious Abe no Yoritoki, whom Sadato succeeded as head of the clan when Yoritoki was killed in 1057. Sadato then took up the reins of the military efforts against the Minamoto. His first notable success came at Kawasaki where he battled through heavy snow to win a victory. Other battles followed, during which Sadato's attacks, along with the harsh weather and terrain, weakened his enemies. As the war drew on, however, he faced a progressively stronger enemy. In 1062, at his fort at Kuriyagawa he was forced to stand. For several days Sadato and his men held out but soon, besieged, with the crucial water supply cut off, and the fortress around him aflame, the Abe leader was compelled to surrender. His

head was paraded through Kyoto by the returning Minamoto the following year.

**Above:** A triptych from Abe Sadato's life as shown in a night-time scene from a Kabuki play: Abe Sadato (center), his wife Sadato Tsuma Sodehagi (left), and (right), holding a parasol, Hachiman Taro Yoshiie. *Library of Congress Prints and Photographs Division*

# Akechi Mitsuhide
(c. 1528–1582)
Sengoku era general

**Above:** Akechi Mitsuhide dies at the hands of a peasant. *via CS*
**Above right:** Akechi Mitsuharu crossing Lake Biwa to kill the wife and children of Akechi Mitsuhide. *via Clive Sinclaire*
**Below right:** Akechi Mitsuhide reviews his troops. *British Museum/Jo St Mart*

Akechi Mitsuhide was a Sengoku era general, and along with Katsuie Shibata, Hideyoshi Toyotomi, one of Nobunaga's close circle of retainers. However, he has achieved notoriety for eventual betraying his erstwhile master at the Honnoji in 1582.

Mitsuhide was born in Mino province (now Gifu prefecture) into the Akechi family, and was thus able to able to trace his heritage to the Toki and from there to the Minamoto. He entered Nobunaga's service after the latter's campaign in Mino province in 1566. For his service in this campaign he was awarded the Sakamoto domain (Omi) in 1571. Subsequently he pacified the Tamba region and the Hatano clan. In 1579, he took over Yakami castle from Hatano Hideharu through a peaceful settlement. Nobunaga, however, rescinded on this agreement, and Hideharu was summarily executed, leading several of

Hideharu's retainers to murder Akechi Mitsuhide's mother. A schism developed between Mitsuhide and Nobunaga over this incident and eventually led Mitsuhide to exact his revenge with the infamous attack at Honnoji on June 21, 1582.

The exact details of Oda Nobunaga's death are unclear, and although it is often stated that Mitsuhide killed Oda Nobunaga, in fact it seems he forced him to commit *seppuku*. In the aftermath of the incident many of Mitsuhide's allies renounced him. Two weeks after burning Honnoji, Mitsuhide was defeated by Toyotomi Hideyoshi at the battle of Yamazaki. Mitsuhide is rumored to have been killed by a peasant warrior with a bamboo spear. Another rumor is that he was not killed at all, escaped and had entered the priesthood under the name Tenkai.

明智左馬之助湖水渡

**Above right:** Akechi Hidemitsu was one of Mitsuhides staunchest retainers. Married to one of Mitsuhides daughters, he led the attack that killed Oda Nobunaga and understood only too well what would happen following his masters defeat by Hideyoshi at Yamazaki. So, after the battle, he rode furiously to Sakamoto Castle, crossing Lake Biwa as seen here, to kill the wives and families of Akechi Mitsuhide and his supporters rather than let them fall into Hideyoshis hands.. Note the flag bearing the Akechi mon. *via Clive Sinclaire*

**Right:** Akechi Mitsuhide served under Nobunaga at his great victory over the Takeda at Nagashino.

俗名 中村玉助

宗讃日徳居士

月元五日 行年六十一戈

津中寺町 正法寺

# Amako Haruhisa
(1514–1561)
Sengoku era *daimyo*

Amako Haruhisa was a Sengoku era *daimyo* whose efforts greatly expanded the Amako domain. Haruhisa was the eldest son of Amako Masahisa and the grandson of Amako Tsunehisa. Like many of his peers Haruhisa changed his name. Known first as Akihisa, he became Haruhisa in 1541.

In 1518 Haruhisa's father was killed while laying siege to the castle of a rebellious Amako retainer, Sakurai Soteki. Haruhisa was then placed in the care of his uncle, Amako Kunihisa, who acted as his guardian until he came of age.

Soon after he assumed control of the Amako in 1537, he began efforts to expand Amako influence eastward, taking valuable silver mines in Itami and then in 1538 moving on Harima province where he fought the Akamatsu at Ojio and Akashi castles. In 1540 he gathered an army of some 30,000 men for an attack on the Mori of Aki province at their Koriyama stronghold. However, despite a significant numerical advantage his siege failed, and Haruhisa was forced to retreat in the face of a counterattack by Mori Motonari.

Battles with the Ouchi clan occupied Haruhisa in the early 1540s, starting with his successful defense of Gassan-Toda against Ouchi in 1542–43. The overthrow of Ouchi Yoshitaka by Sue Harukata in 1551 confirmed his dominance in the area east of Izumo. By 1552 Haruhisa, and the Amako were at the height of their power, confirmed by official acknowledgment from *shogun* Ashikaga Yoshiteru of their pre-eminence in Izumo, Bingo, Bizen, Bittchu, Hoki, Inaba, Mimasaka, and Oki Island.

However, the Amako became split

**Left:** Amako Haruhisa at his height controlled Izumo, Bingo, Bizen, Bittchu, Hoki, Inaba, Mimasaka, and Oki Island. *British Museum/Jo St Mart*

**Right:** Asai Nagamasa fought against his brother-in-law Oda Nobunaga at the battle of Anegawa in 1570. *British Museum/Jo St Mart*

into two factions, one of them centering Haruhisa and the other, the "Shingu faction," surrounding Amako Kunihisa. The Shingu faction included many of the senior officers in the Amako army and was thus a threat to Haruhisa's power. In 1554 he moved to quash this threat and consolidate his authority over the Amako, ordering the murder of Kunihisa, his son Sanehisa, and various other members of the Shingu faction. Between 1556 and his sudden death at Gassan-Toda in January 1561 Haruhisa battled Mori Motonari for control of Iwami Province. Although Haruhisa held on to the silver mines, Motonari seized the eastern part of the province. He was succeeded by his son Yoshihisa.

## Asai Nagamasa
### (1545–1573)
### Sengoku era *daimyo* and general

Asai Nagamasa was a Sengoku era *daimyo* and general, noted for his opposition to Oda Nobunaga. He was born at Odani castle and was the son of Asai Hisamasa (1524–1573), the second *daimyo* of the Asai family, whose power-base was in northern Omi Province, east of Lake Biwa.

At a young age, a marriage of expediency was arranged for Nagamasa with a girl of the Rokkaku clan, but after traveling to Kannonji Nagamasa declined the proposed union and returned to Odani. So, in 1560, when just fifteen years old, Nagamasa inherited the leadership of the Asai from his father, after the latter had been pressed into relinquishing his position by those who had his ear. Hisamasa acquiesced and retired to live a quiet life at Odani.

In the following years Nagamasa sought to break away from the Rokkaku, and in so doing proved to be a competent if not outstanding leader. His first major battle in command was the battle of Norada in 1560, where he heavily defeated a Rokkaku army led by Yoshikata, who was currently trying to consolidate his power through subjugation of the Asai. Subsequently, Nagamasa successfully battled both Rokkaku Yoshikata and Saito Tatsuoki on a number of occasions.

In 1564 he married Oda Nobunaga's sister Oichi, a union Nobunaga engineered to ensure cordial relations with the Asai because of the strategic position they occupied near to Kyoto. However, in 1570, Oda Nobunaga declared war on the Asakura family of Echizen, an old Asai ally. The clan became divided between those who wished to honor the alliance with the Asakura, and others, including Nagamasa himself, who favored staying neutral, essentially siding with Nobunaga. In the end, the Azai clan chose to honor alliance with the Asakura, prompting Nobunaga to call off his march on the Asakura domain. However, in the summer of 1570, Nobunaga and Tokugawa Ieyasu brought an army estimated between 20–30,000 men into Northern Omi to confront an allied Asai/Asakura force. In midsummer the two sides met at the battle of Anegawa. The battle ended indecisively, but over the course of the next two years, Asai Nagamasa was under constant threat of Nobunaga aggression into Omi and his castle at Odani. In 1573, Oda laid siege to Odani again. An Asakura relief force was defeated and chased back to their lands. Shortly thereafter, Nobunaga returned south to prosecute the siege of Odani.

In August, faced with imminent collapse of his defenses, Nagamasa sent his three daughters and his wife, Nobunaga's sister out of the castle. They were allowed to live. He then led one last assault on Nobunaga's camp, but was captured and allowed to commit *seppuku* along with his young son.

## Asakura Norikage
### (1477–1555)
### Sengoku era general, politician, and writer

Asakura Norikage was a Sengoku era general, politician, and writer on military matters, and one of the most powerful figures in the early Sengoku period. He was the eighth son of Asakura Toshikage, and entered the priesthood under the name Soteki. In 1503 his nephew Sadakage became *daimyo*, fomenting a plot by certain Asakura retainers that Norikage was approached to join. Norikage consented to join the conspirators, but on the eve of the attempted coup he revealed all to his nephew. Sadakage promptly ordered an army to attack Tsuruga castle, the seedbed of the opposition, and forced its ringleader Asakura Kagefusa to flee to Echizen.

As the one of the Asakura's leading military commanders Norikage won a number of notable victories. At Kuzuryugawa in 1506 he defeated the *Ikko-ikki* and led expeditions into Tango province. Norikage lent support to the Asai against the expanding power of the Rokkaku in 1526, cementing mutual cooperation between them for further operations against the troublesome *Ikko-ikki* rebels in the province of Kaga in 1531. At the battle of Daishojiomote in 1555, Norikage fell ill forcing him to personally retreat back to Ichijodani, and ceding command of the Asakura army to Asakura Kagetaka. He died on September 23, 1555, to be succeeded by his adopted nephew, Kagetoshi, as clan head. Posthumously he was held in regard as the finest general that the Asakura possessed. Many of his extensive writings on military matters survive, along with many sayings attributed to him.

**Right:** Asakura Norikage left an invaluable written record about military matters, including the thought: "The warrior may be called a beast or a dog; the main thing is winning." *British Museum/Jo St Mart*

beauty. In the mid-sixteenth century, it was also a place of refuge for courtiers fleeing the relentless turmoil of Kyoto, adding to the sense of refinement.

But away from the cosseted world of Ichijodani, life was not always so tranquil. Beginning in 1565, Yoshikage became embroiled in a plot that would eventually cost him his life. The *shogun*, Yoshiteru, was assassinated and Yoshikage shortly received call to arms from Yoshiteru's brother and successor, Yoshiaki. Although he was regent, Yoshikage vacillated over his course of action. Yoshiaki appealed instead to Oda Nobunaga, and with his assistance, was installed as the fifteenth Ashikaga *shogun* in 1568.

Under Nobunaga, however, Yoshiaki's position of authority was never more than titular and he soon grew restive. Consequently, he began to correspond in secret with various *daimyo*, soliciting their support for a scheme to expel Nobunaga. Nobunaga's spies soon got details of this correspondence and, fearing Yoshikage might answer Yoshiaki's call, he preemptively invaded Echizen.

The Asai of Omi promptly raised an army to alleviate the pressure on Yoshikage. Nevertheless, he was defeated at the battle of Anegawa, prompting him to seek a firmer alliance with the Asai. However,

# Asakura Yoshikage
## (1533–73)
**Sengoku era *daimyo*, court regent and aesthete**

Asakura Yoshikage was a Sengoku era *daimyo*, court regent and aesthete from Echizen. He assumed leadership of the clan from his father, Asakura Takakage, in 1548. At that time Echizen was endangered by *Ikko-ikki* uprisings in neighboring Kaga, but Yoshikage was able to build a relatively secure position in the territories centering on his stronghold at Ichijodani.

Ichijodani, much of which has today been restored to its former glories, stands as a testament to Yoshikage's devotion to art and

Nobunaga surrounded and attacked the Asai stronghold at Odani castle and the fledgling coalition was quickly destroyed. Yoshikage himself escaped and returned to Ichijodani, but was betrayed there by his cousin, Kageaki, and forced to commit *seppuku*.

## Ashikaga Takauji
### (1305–1358)
### First *shogun* of the Ashikaga Shogunate

Ashikaga Takauji was the first shogun of the Ashikaga shogunate, the administration of which he was founder and which he ruled for twenty years from 1338. He is a central character in the epic *Taiheiki*, the classic account of the Muromachi period of Japan.

Takauji's lineage can be traced back to the Seiwa Minamoto, of Shimotsuke Province (in present-day Tochigi Prefecture). He entered military service at an unknown age, but by 1333 he was a general in the army of the Kamakura shogunate. He was subsequently charged with extinguishing the so-called Genko Rebellion in Kyoto, and with the exiled Emperor Go-Daigo and Kusunoki Masashige, Takauji conspired to seize Kyoto, with the aim of reestablishing the power of the imperial court (the Kemmu Restoration).

However the popularity of Go-Daigo's new administration quickly soured, and within a short time, many samurai clans had grown disillusioned with his program of reforms. Voices of discontent were raised, and sensing the growing restlessness, Takauji pleaded with the emperor to address the crisis before rebellion broke out. His warnings were not heeded.

In 1335, these dissatisfactions instigated the Nakasendai rebellion (*Nakasendai no ran*), an attempt to reestablish the shogunate at Kamakura. Takauji quickly put down the rebellion and took Kamakura for himself. He then claimed the title of *seii tai shogun* and began allotting land to his followers without due authority from the court. Takauji announced his allegiance to the imperial court, but Go-Daigo sent an army under Nitta Yoshisada to reclaim Kamakura.

At the battle of Hakone Take, Takauji defeated Yoshisada, and subsequently occupied Kyoto for a brief time. However, he was quickly forced

**Above:** Samurai warrior Ashikaga Takauji became *shogun* and opened his *bakufu* at Muromachi, Kyoto. Under his rule the economy prospered as did the merchants and peasants. *British Museum/Jo St Mart*

to quit the capital and retreat to Kyushu by Go-Daigo's forces.

In Kyushu, Takauji allied himself with local clans and again marched to Kyoto. At the battle of Minato River in 1336, Takauji decisively defeated Go-Daigo's forces, allowing him to seize Kyoto for good. Thus began the Northern and Southern Court Period (*Nanboku-cho*), which would endure for almost sixty years.

Ashikaga Takauji's son, Ashikaga Yoshiakira, succeeded him as *shogun* after his death. His grandson Ashikaga Yoshimitsu united the Northern and Southern courts in 1392.

## Ashikaga Tadayoshi
### (1306–1352)
### General of the Northern and Southern Courts

Ashikaga Tadayoshi was a general during the Nanboku-cho period, and a key ally of Go-Daigo and his better known elder brother Ashikaga Takauji (during the Nakasendai Rebellion). Tadayoshi lent his support to Go-Daigo in the Kemmu Restoration of 1333 and for this he was rewarded given the position of governor (*kami*) of Sagami Province (now part of Kanagawa Prefecture). Within two years he had turned against the emperor and in 1335,

**Above**: Ashikaga Takauji closing with the enemy on the field of battle. *via Clive Sinclaire*

played a leading role in the Nakasendai rebellion. He captured the emperor's son—Prince Morinaga—whom he held captive in a cave near Kamakura for some nine months before executing him. The following year Tadayoshi helped to install a rival monarch and with his brother founded the Muromachi shogunate in 1338. Under this new bakufu, Takauji took charge of military affairs and Tadayoshi of judicial and administrative matters.

Some years later, in 1350, a major conflict broke out with his brother's

**Right:** Ashikaga Yoshiaki was the abbot of the Ichijoin in Nara before leaving to take up arms and challenge for his murdered brother Ashikaga Yoshiteru's position of *shogun*. *British Museum/Jo St Mart*

deputy, Ko no Moronao. Tadayoshi took up arms in protest, and in 1351 he occupied Kyoto. This incident, commonly referred to as the Kanno Disturbance, dragged on for the best part of two years. There was a brief reconciliation with Takauji but this cracked and they once again fell to squabbling.

By March 1352 Tadayoshi and his retinue had been pursued to Kamakura. At this juncture there was another brief sibling reconciliation, but shortly thereafter Tadayoshi died, suddenly in what were suspicious circumstances. There is speculation that he was poisoned.

## Ashikaga Yoshiaki
### (1537–1597)
### Ashikaga *shogun*

Ashikaga Yoshiaki was the fifteenth Ashikaga *shogun*, and an key political opponent to Oda Nobunaga. In 1562 his brother, Yoshiteru was assassinated by agents of the Miyoshi and Matsunaga clans. Seeking vengeance for his death, Yoshiaki convinced Oda Nobunaga to march on Kyoto in the autumn of 1568, and was installed as the fifteenth Ashikaga *shogun*. However, Yoshiaki soon grew tired of Nobunaga and there was a marked and rapid decline in relations between the two men. In early 1573 he took advantage of Nobunaga's preoccupation with Takeda Shingen and issued a call for rebellion to the Asai, Asakura, and Takeda. In May Nobunaga surrounded Kyoto, and Yoshikai sued for peace. However, in the summer Yoshiaki rose up again, establishing his forces at a stronghold on the Uji River called Makinoshima. After a short siege, Yoshiaki surrendered on August 18. Subsequently he was banished from Kyoto, marking the end of the Ashikaga Shogunate. He died in Osaka in the fall of 1597.

## Baba Nobuharu
**(1514–1575)**
**Sengoku military commander**

Baba Nobuharu was a Sengoku era military commander, a trusted adviser to Takeda Shingen and one of his band of "Twenty-Four Generals." Nobuharu's clan, the Kai Baba, was descended from Minamoto Yorimitsu and had served as retainers to the Takeda clan for generations. In all he fought in twenty-one battles—apparently without receiving a single wound—but his most famous actions were at Mikatagahara (1573) and Nagashino (1575), where he met his death in close combat. Following the destruction of the Takeda in 1582, one branch of the Baba survived to serve Tokugawa Ieyasu.

**Right**: Baba Nobuharu died in battle at Nagashino in 1582, apparently without ever having received a wound before. *British Museum/Jo St Mart*

## Chosogabe Motochika
### (1538–1599)
#### Sengoku Period *daimyo*

Chosokabe Motochika was a Sengoku Period *daimyo*, whose stronghold was in the southern Shikoku province of Tosa (present-day Kochi Prefecture). Under Motochika the Chosokabe clan steadily expanded across Shikoku. In 1575, he was victorious at the battle of Shimantogawa (near present day Shimanto City), against Ichijo Kanesada, and in the process gained control of all of Tosa. Over the ensuing decade, he extended his power to all of Shikoku. However, in 1585, Toyotomi Hideyoshi arrived on Shikoku with an overwhelming force of 100,000 men and some of his best generals. Motochika was faced with little choice but to surrender, and give up Awa, Sanuki, and Iyo provinces, although he was allowed to retain Tosa.

Under Hideyoshi, Motochika and his son Nobuchika participated in the campaign in Kyushu, during which Nobuchika was killed. In 1590, Motochika led a fleet in the siege of Odawara, and also fought in the Japanese invasions of Korea in 1592. Motochika died in 1599 at age sixty-one at his mansion in Fushimi.

# Date Masamune
## (1567–1636)
### Late Azuchi-Momoyama and early Edo Period *daimyo*

Date Masamune was a *daimyo* of the late Azuchi-Momoyama and early Edo Period. Instantly recognizable for the eye-patch he wore to cover his right eye—lost to smallpox at a young age—and crescent-moon helmet, Masamune was the consummate military man, an outstanding tactician and possessed of single-minded ruthlessness. The "one-eyed dragon" or *dokuganryu* as he was known, was the eldest son of Date Terumune, born in Yonezawa castle (in modern Yamagata Prefecture).

In 1581, when only fourteen years old, Masamune campaigned with his father, Terumune, against the Soma family, and three years later succeeded him as *daimyo*. Disregarding former alliances he then began to attack and conquer territories surrounding the Date fief. After defeating the Ashina in 1589, he made Aizu domain his base of operations.

By 1590 Date could no longer ignore the authority of Toyotomi Hideyoshi when the latter compelled the Tohoku *daimyos* to lend their support to his operations. Masamune initially refused, incurring Hideyoshi's wrath, and nearly paid for his recalcitrance with his life. However, Hideyoshi spared him and after was given Iwatesawa castle and the surrounding lands. Under Masamune's steerage the region became a major political and economic center.

In 1592 Masamune led men in the campaign on the Korean peninsula, during which he earned some reputation. After Hideyoshi's death, he lent his weight to Tokugawa Ieyasu and for this he was made lord of the huge and profitable Sendai domain. As lord of Sendai Masamune was, effectively, one of Japan's most powerful *daimyo*.

In Sendai, he built many palaces and worked on many projects to improve the region. Unusually, he also encouraged foreigners to come to his land, showing sympathy for Christian missionaries and traders. However, it is likely he was primarily motivated by a desire for foreign technology, and when Tokugawa Ieyasu outlawed Christianity, Masamune quickly followed suit.

Masamune was an important sponsor of the few diplomatic expeditions and voyages of exploration emanating from Japan in this period, sending an embassy via the Philippines, Mexico, and Spain to establish relations with the Pope in Rome. This voyage was first Japanese circumnavigation of the globe.

**Left:** Date Masamune's equestrian statue is located in Sendai, the city he founded.
*Michael S. Yamashita/Corbis*

# Date Terumune
## (1543–1585)
### Date clan *daimyo*

Date Terumune was *daimyo* of the Date clan during the late Sengoku period of feudal Japan. Despite his aversion to Terumune, Date Harumune was fearful that the Ashikaga would try and destroy his clan, and therefore ceded his position as leader to his son Terumune around the year 1560. Terumune thus became the sixteenth head.

With the tacit support of the current head of the Ashikaga, Ashikaga Yoshiteru, the young ruler expanded his territory over thirty districts by the age of seventeen. Terumune also established cordial relations with Oda Nobunaga and was held in high regard by his retainers as a resolution. After nearly a quarter century as head of his clan, Terumune stepped aside to let his son, Masamune, succeed.

Sometime later, at a council with the head of his erstwhile enemy Hatakeyama Yoshitsugu, he was suddenly taken hostage, and spirited away to a Hatekeyama fortress. An unconfirmed story has it that Masumune intercepted the hostage party, and at this, disregarding his own life, Terumune ordered his son to open fire. Terumune was killed along with Yoshitsugu. Another version exists that Yoshitsugu survived the incident and died a year later when the Hatekeyama fortress was besieged.

**Left:** Date Terumune was seventeen when he became the Date clan *daimyo* even though he did not have a warlike disposition; he was, however, very popular with many of his retainers. *British Museum/Jo St Mart*

**Right:** Wounded samurai following the battle of Ueno (July 4, 1868). After the battle Prince Yoshihisa escaped and reached Enomoto Takeaki's warship, but Takeaki had to surrender in the end and accept the Meiji emperor's rule. *Asian Art & Archaeology, Inc./Corbis*

## Enomoto Takeaki
### (1836–1908)
### Naval admiral of the Tokugawa Shogunate

Viscount Enomoto Takeaki was a naval admiral in the final days of the Tokugawa Shogunate, and later the head of the short-lived Ezo Republic. As a member of the Meiji government he helped to found the Imperial Japanese Navy.

Enomoto was born into a samurai retainer family of the Tokugawa clan in Edo (modern Tokyo). He spent time in Europe from 1862 to 1867 studying naval warfare and securing contracts for western technologies and was promoted to *kaigun fukuso-sai*, the second highest rank in the Tokugawa Navy, at the age of thirty-one.

At the climax of the 1868 Boshin War, he led the remainder of the Tokugawa Navy fleet to Hakodate in Hokkaido after the fall of the Edo shogunate. With other Tokugawa loyalists, Enomoto attempted to establish an independent country (the Ezo Republic) in Hokkaido, and was elected its first president.

The next year, however, the Meiji government forces invaded Hokkaido and defeated Enomoto's forces at sea in the battle of Hakodate. The Republic of Ezo collapsed, and Enomoto was arrested, accused of high treason and imprisoned. He was subsequently pardoned and using his political skills, rose quickly to prominence within the new ruling clique. In 1880, Enomoto

became Navy Minister, and held various posts culminating in Foreign Minister from 1891–1892. Enomoto died in 1908 at the age of seventy-two.

**Left:** A Kubuki actor represents Enomoto Takeaki. After spending six years in the Netherlands he became vice president of the Shogunate Navy. This foreign education later became useful to him and his country. *British Museum/Jo St Mart*

# Fujiwara Kiyohira
## (1056–1128)
## Samurai and Fujiwara dynasty founder

Fujiwara Kiyohira was a late Heian period samurai, and founder of the Fujiwara dynasty (*Hiraizumi*) that ruled Mutsu from about 1100 to 1226.

Kiyohira was the son of Fujiwara no Tsunekiyo, a middle-ranking official at Taga castle (in present-day Sendai, Miyagi Prefecture) who left his post to live with the unidentified Emishi woman who was Kiyohira's mother. During the Early Nine Years War (*Zenkunen*) he lost his father (personally beheaded by Minamoto no Yoriyoshi himself), his grandfather Abe no Yoritoki, his uncle Sadato; all of his mother's brothers were deported to Kyushu. Subsequently, the Kiyohara clan brought up Kiyohira, together with his elder brother-in-law Sanehira and younger half-brother Iehira. Infighting between these three siblings instigated the Later Three Years War from which Kiyohira emerged as the victor in 1087.

**Above:** Following victory in the Later Three Years War, Kiyohira returned home to Fort Toyoda but soon built a new home on Mount Kanzan (Barrier Mountain); this was the start of present day Hiraizumi Town. *British Museum/Jo St Mart*

35

Kiyohira returned to his home at Toyota castle, Mutsu (present-day Iwate), and built a new home on Mount Kanzan, in what is now Hiraizumi Town. He also initiated an ambitious building program on the top of Mount Kanzan, the Chosen-ji, a complex of temples, pagodas, repositories, and gardens.

# Fujiwara no Sumitomo
## (d. 941)
### Heian era noble, warrior, and pirate

Fujiwara no Sumitomo was a Heian era court noble, warrior, and pirate. Little is known of his early life, beyond that his father was Fujiwara no Yoshinori, and thus an ancestor of the Arima *daimyo* family of Hizen province.

Sumitomo was originally a government official, and in this capacity the court dispatched him to eliminate pirates plaguing the Inland Sea, which connects central and southern Japan. However, Sumitomo betrayed the trust placed in him and became leader of the pirates and other dissident local bands. Basing himself at Hiburijima Island (near Sada Misaki in present day Ehime prefecture), he gained control of most of the strategic waters surrounding the western end of the Inland Sea. In 939, he led a revolt in Iyo province, and soon afterwards invaded the provinces of

Harima and Bizen. The revolt quickly spread throughout the whole San'yo region. Pursued by imperial forces, Sumitomo fled to Dazaifu, and was defeated in battle at Hakata. He then fled back to Iyo province, where in 941 he was captured, and executed.

**Above:** Sumitomo became a revolutionary leader, initially in Iyo province, then throughout the entire Sanyo region. He was eventually captured back in Iyo and quickly executed. *British Museum/Jo St Mart*

**Right:** Fujiwara Nobuyori arranged a palace coup and imprisoned both the emperor and ex-emperor: this briefly brought him power but when they were freed by supporters, Nobuyori paid with his life. *British Museum/Jo St Mart*

# Fujiwara Nobuyori
## (d. 1160)
### Influential Heian era courtier

Fujiwara no Nobuyori was a late Heian era courtier and one of the chief allies of Minamoto no Yoshitomo in the Heiji Rebellion of 1159.

During the Heian era (794–1185), four great families dominated Japanese politics, and the Fujiwara was one of the most important of them. The Fujiwara had established a hereditary claim to the position of regent, either for the *sessho* (infant) or *kampaku* (adult) emperor. Nobuyori had ambitions for this position, but was overshadowed at court by Fujiwara no Michinori, who enjoyed influence and privileges which Fujiwara no Nobuyori could only envy. In the late 1150s, a dispute arose between the followers of the reigning Emperor Nijo and those who favored the retired (cloistered) Emperor Go-Shirakawa. Though Fujiwara Michinori and the Taira clan supported Nijo, Nobuyori and his Minamoto allies supported Go-Shirakawa's bid to retain some influence and power. Nobuyori saw this as an opportunity to advance his cause, and gathered around him a faction of supporters, including members of the Minamoto clan.

In early 1160, Michinori's ally Taira no Kiyomori departed Kyoto, providing Nobuyori's faction with the opportunity they needed. Together they attacked and burned the Sanjo Palace, and abducted both Emperor Nijo and the cloistered Emperor

Go-Shirakawa. They then turned on Michinori, destroying his home and killing all those inside, with the exception of Michinori himself, who escaped only to be captured and beheaded soon afterward.

Nobuyori then forced Nijo to appoint him chancellor. His reign was all but brief, as Taira no Kiyomori returned to the capital and, finding the usurpers insufficiently prepared, quickly retook it. The emperor and ex-emperor were both freed, the Minamoto defeated, and Nobuyori killed.

## Fujiwara Yorinaga
### (1120–1156)
### Later Heian era court official

Fujiwara no Yorinaga was a high-ranking court official in the later Heian era, and one of the major insti-gators of the Hogen rebellion. He ascended quickly through the political ranks and held the position of *naidaijin* (minister of the center) by the age of seventeen. In 1150, he was appointed *sadaijin* (minister of the left), second only to the *daijo daijin* (chancellor) in rank under the regent.

However, Yorinaga opposed the appointment in 1142 of Emperor, Konoe, and the controlling influence

**Right:** Fujiwara Yorinaga fought against the Go-Shirakawa party. He was one of the last major advocates in favor of restoring the once powerful Fujiwara Regency. *British Museum/Jo St Mart*

the cloistered Emperor Toba had over him. In 1155, Konoe died and a succession dispute arose for the imperial throne. After much disagreement, and to Yorinaga's disquiet, Toba's son Go-Shirakawa was appointed. Yorinaga joined forces with former emperor Sutoku, one of Toba's other sons and began to assemble an army of troops collected from outer provinces, with the goal of marching on the capital. However, Yorinaga was only able to muster a few hundred soldiers with which to carry through his plan to topple Go-Shirakawa, who had the substantial backing of both the Minamoto and Taira warrior clans. In the event, Sutoku and Yorinaga were defeated and Yorinaga was killed, a symbolic beginning for the growth of the samurai class.

## Fukushima Masanori
**(1561–1624)**
**One of the Seven Spears of Shizugatake**

One of Hideyoshi's retainers, he fought in the battle of Shizugatake in 1583, and thereafter was known as one of the Seven Spears of Shizugatake. He fought through the Kanto campaign (1590), the Korean Campaign (1592), and at Sekigahara, supporting Tokugawa Ieyasu after Hideyoshi's death in 1598. Ieyasu, however, was never completely sure of him—and neither, after Ieyasu's death in 1616—was the new *shogun*, Hidetada.

**Left:** Fukushima Masanori was rewarded for his support of Toyotomi Hideyoshi throughout the Shizugatake Campaign with a gift of land worth 5,000 koku. *via Clive Sinclaire*

## Hashiba Hidenaga
### (1540–1591)
### Sengoku era general

Hashiba Hidenaga was a Sengoku era general and a close confidante of Toyotomi Hideyoshi.

Although he was born Hidenaga he later assumed the Toyotomi name of his illustrious half-brother Hideyoshi, with whom he shared maternal ties. Hidenaga joined Hideyoshi's staff when the latter took up in Omi province in 1573. Following Oda Nobunaga's death in 1582 and the defeat of Akechi Mitsuhide, he was given the fief of Koriyama in Yamato (confiscated from the Tsutsui). In 1585 Hideyoshi charged Hidenaga with leading the campaign against Chosogabe Motochika in Shikoku, and subsequently gave him command of 60,000 men for the invasion of Kyushu in 1587.

Hidenaga's prosecution of the campaign was cautious, despite the comparative weakness of the Shimazu resistance, but nonetheless thorough. Afterward, Hidenaga acted as guardian to Hideyoshi's son Tsurumatsu. However, when Tsurumatsu died in 1591, leaving Hideyoshi without an heir, it seemed

**Right:** Hashiba Hidenaga assumed the name Toyotomi of his half-brother Hideyoshi (right; see also pages 172-176). *The Art Archive*

likely that Hidenaga would be chosen to succeed. Unfortunately, Hidenaga finally succumbed that year to an illness that had dogged him for a number of years. Hideyoshi, it seems, felt his loss greatly.

## Hatakeyama Shigetada
### (1164–1205)
**Samurai who fought in Genpei Wars**

Shigetada was a samurai famed for his bravery. He fought for the Taira clan but changed sides on April 25, 1185, at the great sea battle of Dan-no-ura. *The Tale of the Heike*—the epic account of the struggle between the Taira and Minamoto clans in the Genpei Wars—identifies him as one of the samurai who competed to be the first across the Uji River. His end was as a result of the politics of the time: Hojo Tokimasa was convinced that Hatakeyama Shigetada was inciting rebellion in Kyoto against him and ordered him killed.

**Right:** Hatakeyama Shigetada, riddled with arrows, rides from the battlefield after being attacked by the mutinous troops of his Lord Tokimasa. From the series *Yoshitoshi mushaburui* (Yoshitoshi's Finest Warriors). *Asian Art & Archaeology, Inc./Corbis*

將源義久卿

## Hatakayama Yoshitsugu
**(1552–1586)**
**Sengoku era** *daimyo*

Hatakeyama Yoshitsugu was a Sengoku era *daimyo* and head of the Hatakeyama clan of Mutsu. He assumed leadership of the clan from his father Hatakeyama Yoshikuni during the later Sengoku period in the 1560s, and had frequent clashes with the Date and Ashina over control of Mutsu. Yoshitsugu attempted to make peace with Date Masamune after 1584, but failed and he instead attempted to kidnap Date Terumune. The plan went wrong and Terumune was killed. Following this incident, Yoshitsugu was besieged for many months and eventually surrendered, only to be put to death by Masumune in revenge.

## Hojo Soun
**(1432–1519)**
*Daimyo* **and founder of the Go-Hojo clan**

Hojo Soun was a Sengoku era *daimyo* and the first head of the Go-Hojo clan. There is much speculation about his early life, some sources say he was born in Kyoto while others cite Bitchu. He was born into a family of Taira lineage that had little importance or power and was known during his lifetime by the name Ise Shinkuro. Originally it seems he was a samurai or *ronin*, yet through family connections (his sister was married to Imagawa Yoshitada), he was able to climb within the Imagawa clan to a position of considerable power. Upon Yoshitada's death in 1476, a succession dispute broke out between Yoshitada's son Imagawa Ujichika and Yoshitada's cousin, Oshika Norimitsu, in which Shinkuro mediated. Ultimately, he sided with Ujichika and killed Norimitsu, for which he had Kokukuji castle. He wrested control of Izu Province in 1493, an act which as led him to be regarded by most historians as the first of the Sengoku era *daimyo*.

Soun went on to capture territory in Sagami, taking Odawara, Kamakura, in 1512, and the castle of Arai in 1518. Soun died the following year, and was succeeded by his son Ujitsuna, who subsequently changed the clan name to the illustrious Hojo and posthumously renamed his father to Hojo Soun. In addition his skills as a politician and general, Soun was a thorough and capable administrator, well-liked and respected by the common people over whom he governed

From the *Soun-ji Dono Nijuichi Kajo* (c.1495), (The Twenty-One Articles of Lord Soun)

*"Don't think your swords and clothes should be as good as those of other people. Be content as long as they don't look awful. Once you start acquiring what you don't have and become even poorer, you'll become a laughing stock."*

*"Whenever you have a little bit of time for yourself, read a book. Always carry something with characters written on it with you and look at it when no one's looking. Unless you accustom yourself to them, asleep or awake, you'll forget them. The same is true of writing."*

*"There's they saying, 'Do everything with others, and you'll have no trouble.' Rely on others in everything."*

*"When you have to walk past the elders lined up in the corridor for the master's audience, you must bend at the hips and lower your hands. It's absolutely out of the question not to show deference or humility but to stomp past. All samurai must behave humbly, deferentially."*

*"Anyone without any knowledge of tanka composition must be said to be untalented and shallow. Study it."*

*"Always work at reading, writing, martial skills, archery, and horse riding. There is no need to detail this. Hold literary skills in your left hand, martial skills in your right. This is the law from ancient times. Never neglect it."*

# Hojo Tokimasa
## (1138–1215)
### Kamakura *bakufu shikken* (regent)

Hojo Tokimasa was the *shikken* (regent) during the Kamakura *bakufu*, between 1199 and 1205. He was born in Izu province and rose to become head of the influential Hojo clan. He distanced the clan from the on court succession disputes that fomented the Hogen and Heiji rebellions. However, as a result of the Minamoto's defeat in the latter, Minamoto no Yoritomo was sent to Tokimasa's domain, Izu, in exile. In 1180, Yoritomo wed Tokimasa's daughter, Masako. That same year, the Genpei War broke out and Tokimasa threw the support of the Hojo clan behind the Minamoto.

Five years later after the Minamoto emerged as victors in the Genpei Wars, Hojo no Tokimasa was now in a advantageous position and head of one of the most powerful families in Japan—he was the father-in-law of the *shogun*. In 1199, *shogun* Minamoto no Yoritomo was succeeded by his eighteen-year-old son and heir, Yoriie. Hojo Tokimasa, was appointed *shikken*, or regent for Yoriie, a position of almost unequalled power and influence in the Kamakura hierarchy. Through Tokimasa's deductiveness and intriguing he forced the abdication of Yoriie, and may well have been behind his murder in 1204. After the death of Yoriie and his brother Ichiman, Tokimasa installed Yoritomo's second son, Minamoto no Sanetomo, as the next *shogun* and in his position as leader of the Mandokoro, continued in his at times ruthless machinations in court affairs.

His downfall came in 1205, when he was implicated in a plot to have *shogun* Sanetomo assassinated. Thereafter, he became a Buddhist monk, and retired from his post of *shikken* and head of the Hojo family. Tokimasa retired to a Buddhist monastery in Kamakura, where he died in 1215.

# Hojo Tokimune
## (1251–1284)
### *Shikken* during the Kamakura Shogunate

Hojo Tokimune was *shikken* (regent) under the Kamakura shogunate, and thus a powerful figure in the political hierarchy of the day. However, he is perhaps best known for masterminding the defense of the country against the Mongol invasions in 1273 and 1281. He is also credited with disseminating the teachings of Zen Buddhism among the warrior class. Tokimune was the eldest son of *shikken* Tokiyori and was personally appointed *shikken* at the age of eighteen. (The Hojo *shikken* had

**Above:** Hojo Tokimasa seated (top left), resting with his samurai during the Genpei War—the late Heian period (1180–1185) conflicts between the Taira and Minamoto clans. The former were defeated to be replaced by the Kamakura shogunate under Minamoto Yoritomo in 1192. *British Museum/Jo St Mart*

**Below:** A fan showing a scene from the Uji River battle. *Sakamoto Photo Research Laboratory/Corbis*

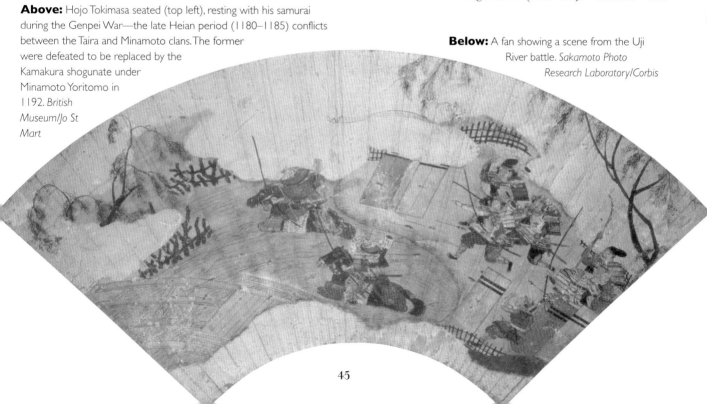

seized power from the Tokugawa *shogun* in 1203 and were the *de facto* rulers of Japan at this time).

Beginning in 1268 he received a series of entreaties from the Mongol Khanate but rejected each of them. He ordered preparations to be made on Kyushu, the most likely target of any landings, and by a measure each of good fortune (the famous *kamikaze*) and skill the first invasion in 1274 was successfully repulsed. When emissaries arrived again in 1275, and 1279, Tokimune responded by having them beheaded. A second invasion attempt in 1281 also failed. Tokimune died three years later.

**Above:** The Mongol war: samurai boats fight the Mongols at sea. *via Clive Sinclaire*

**Right:** Hojo Tokimune was officially the eighth *shikken* (regent) of the Kamakura shogunate, but was in fact the *de facto* ruler at a time when Japan was threatened by the invading Mongols. He became known for extending *Bushido* (the Way of the Warrior) among the samurai and for helping the spread of Zen Buddhism across Japan. *British Museum/Jo St Mart*

# Hojo Ujitsuna
**(1487–1541)**
**Sengoku era** *daimyo*

Hojo Ujitsuna was a *daimyo* of the early Sengoku era , the second head of the Go-Hojo clan. After the death of his father, Soun, Ujitsuna took up his cause and continued to fight for control of the Kanto region. One of his first acts was to seize Edo castle from Uesugi Tomoki, and by this act of aggression touched off a long period of strife between the two clans. Two years later, the Uesugi attacked and burned Kamakura, but were quickly driven out of the Hojo domains. In 1537, when Uesugi Tomoki died, Ujitsuna seized his Kawagoe castle, and finally secured his control of the Kanto. In the final years of his life he secured Shimosa Province and directed the rebuilding of Kamakura, which along with Odawara and Edo, stood thereafter as symbols of Hojo power.

# Hojo Ujiyasu
**(1515–1571)**
**Go-Hojo clan** *daimyo*

Hojo Ujiyasu was the son of Hojo Ujitsuna and the third *daimyo* of the Go-Hojo clan during the Sengoku era. Succeeding his father as head of the clan in 1541, Ujiyasu quickly faced off attempts by rival clans in the Kanto region to seize Hojo strongholds. Ogigayatsu Tomosada was successfully turned back at Edo castle and then, in 1545, an army led by Ashikaga Haruuji and Uesugi Norimasa was seen off at Kawagoe castle

Ujiyasu soon turned to the offensive and in the coming years expanded the Hojo territory over five provinces. One of his most significant gains was Konodai in Shimousa Province, which he took in 1564 from Satomi Yoshihiro. In later years he faced a major threat from Takeda clan under Shingen, before passing away in 1571. The domain passed to his eldest son Hojo Ujimasa.

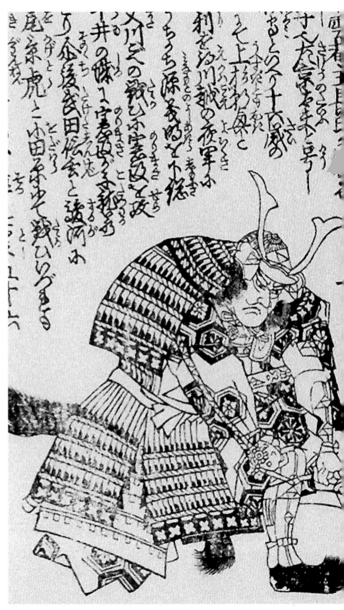

**Above:** Hojo Ujiyasu. *British Museum/Jo St Mart*
**Right:** Hojo Ujitsuna took Edo castle which was under the control of Uesugi Tomoki—beginning the rivalry between the Hojo and the Uesugi families. *British Museum/Jo St Mart*

# Hojo Yasutoki
## (1185–1242)
### *Shikken* during the Kamakura Shogunate

**Left:** Hojo Yoshitoki was the second *shikken* (regent) of the Kamakura Shogunate and head of the Hojo clan. *British Museum/Jo St Mart*

**Below:** Hojo Yasutoki, was the third *shikken* of the Kamakura Shogunate. *British Museum/Jo St Mart*

Hojo Yasutoki, was *shikken* (regent) of the Kamakura Shogunate in Japan between 1224 and 1242, and the architect of much of its legal system. In 1218 he became the *betto* (chief administrator) of the *samurai dokoro* (board of retainers) and in the Jokyu War of 1221, he led the forces of his father, *shogun* Hojo Yoshitoki, against the imperial court of Go-Toba in Kyoto.

After the capture of Kyoto, he remained in the capital and created the post of *Rokuhara Tandai*, whose agencies in Kyoto were responsible for security in Kinai and judicial affairs on western Japan under the Kamakura Shogunate.

There were two *tandai*, one called *kitakata* and the other, lower-ranked, *minamikata*. Yasutoki and his uncle Tokifusa were the first *kitakata* and *minamikata*, respectively.

In 1224 Yoshitoki died and Yasutoki succeeded his father to become *shikken*. Among many reforms of the administrative and judicial system of the *bakufu* he created the post of *rensho* (assistant to the regent), and in 1225 created a council system known as the *hyojo*. He was also the architect of the *goseibai shikimoku* (formulary of adjudications), the legal code of the shogunate, which was introduced to settle land disputes

He died in 1242, to be succeeded as *shikken* by his grandson Tsunetoki.

# Hojo Yoshitoki
## (1163–1224)
### *Shikken* during the Kamakura Shogunate

Hojo Yoshitoki was *shikken* (regent) of the Kamakura Shogunate, from 1205 until his death in 1224, and head of the Hojo clan. He was the eldest son and thus heir of Hojo Tokimasa. In 1179, Yoshitoki's sister Masako married Minamoto no Yoritomo, a union that had the full blessing of the young heir. During the Genpei War, Yoshitoki lent his support to the Minamoto cause

Under *shogun* Minamoto no Yoriie, Yoshitoki, his sister Masako, and father Tokimasa presided over a council of regents to help in ruling the country. However, Yoriie distrusted the Hojo, and in 1203 plotted to have Hojo Tokimasa murdered. But was forced to abdicate in 1203, went to live in Izu, and was executed on Tokimasa's orders in 1204. The following year a schism developed between father and son after Tokimasa ordered the execution of Hatekayama Shigetada, and was implicated in a plot to assassinate *shogun* Minamoto no Sanetomo. Yoshitoki ordered his father to abdicate, and took over his position as *shikken* (regent). His tenure was largely uneventful until in 1218, when Yoshitoki petitioned Cloistered Emperor Go-Toba to allow him to adopt one his sons, Prince Nagahito, as his heir, since he had no children. In 1219, after the assassination of *shogun* Sanetomo, Yoshitoki elevated Kujo Yoritsune, to the position of new *shogun*. Soon, however, Yoshitoki's meddling in court affairs began to rankle with the other courtiers. In 1221, the Cloistered Emperor, Go-Toba, declared *shikken* Yoshitoki an outlaw and ordered him to be executed, triggering the Jokyu War. Yoshitoki ordered his troops to attack Kyoto, and his son and heir Yasutoki took the city in 1222. In 1224, Yoshitoki died at the age of sixty-one years old, to be succeeded as *shikken* by Yasutoki.

# Honda Tadakatsu
## (1548–1610)
### Late Sengoku and early Edo military commander

Honda Tadakatsu was a celebrated military commander under Tokugawa Ieyasu in the late Sengoku and early Edo periods, noted for his bravery in battle and skill in command. In his youth Tadakatsu was one of Ieyasu's pages, rising to become a trusted member of his staff. He fought with distinction on a number of pivotal battles, including Anegawa (1570), Mikatagahara (1573), and Nagashino 1575). He also fought against Toyotomi Hideyoshi in the Komaki Campaign and later received Otaki castle in Kazusa, on the Boso peninsula. He was also present at Sekigahara and afterward received a fief in Izu.

# Hosokawa Katsumoto
## (1430–1473)
### Muromachi era *kanrei*

Hosokawa Katsumoto was a powerful *kanrei* (deputy) to *shogun* Ashikaga Yoshimasa during the Muromachi era. He was one of the main instigators of Onin War, which was itself the catalyst for the 130-year Sengoku *jidai*.

In his position as *kanrei*, Katsumoto enjoyed significant influence, something that was greatly resented by his father-in-law, Yamana Souzen. When Ashikaga Yoshimasa had a son in 1464, a dispute erupted over who would succeed him as *shogun*. Katsumoto favored the *shogun*'s brother Ashikaga Yoshimi, whereas Souzen endorsed the child as rightful heir. In 1467, fighting broke out in the capital Kyoto between Hosokawa's Eastern Army and Yamana's Western Army, each roughly 80,000 strong.

Much of the capital was subsequently destroyed, but within a year the initial fury of the battle had died down and the two forces were thereafter satisfied with sporadic skirmishing. In 1469, the *shogun* named his son Yoshihisa, his heir, but Katsumoto made no response and sued for

**Left:** Honda Tadakatsu was a brave and formidable warrior and called by the powerful *daimyo* Oda Nobunaga—a very hard man to please—"a Samurai among Samurai." *British Museum/Jo St Mart*

**Left:** Hosokawa Katsumoto was in conflict with his father- in-law, Yamana Sozen, who resented the power he had as *kanrei* thus igniting the Onin War of 1467. This civil war started the *Sengoku jidai* (the Warring States Period). *British Museum/Jo St Mart*

**Below:** Hosokawa Tadaoki (center), was the son of Hosokawa Fujitaka. He fought his first battle at the tender age of fifteen under Oda Nobunaga. *British Museum/Jo St Mart*

peace. A satisfactory resolution was agreed, and a few years later, in 1473, both Hosokawa and Yamana died. Kyoto, where they had fought out their battles, took many years to recover. Katsumoto's other lasting legacy is the Ryoan-ji, a Zen temple in north western Kyoto famous for its *karesansui* (dry landscape) rock garden.

# Hosokawa Sumimoto
## (1489–1520)
### Hosokawa Masamoto's appointed heir

The adopted son of Hosokawa Masamoto, Sumimoto became his heir in preference to Hosokawa Sumiyuki, who had been adopted earlier by Sumimoto. Masamoto was

murdered in 1507 by one of Sumiyuki's supporters and Sumimoto was also attacked. He fled. Sumimoto was then helped by Miyoshi Yukinaga (also known as Miyoshi Nagateru) whose troops defeated Sumiyuki.

Sumimoto supported Ashikaga Yoshizumi, whom Masamoto had helped become *shogun* by deposing Ashikaga Yoshiki in 1493. In 1508, supported by Ouchi Yoshioki, Yoshiki was once more installed as *shogun* and Sumimoto fled in the face of a stronger force. In 1511 he returned but was defeated at Funaokayama.

Yoshizumi died on September 6, 1511; but Sumimoto tried once more to defeat Takakuni, this time with Miyoshi Yukinaga. Unfortunately, the supporters of Yoshiki won the day, Yukinaga was defeated and forced to kill himself and Sumimoto fled to Awa where he died shortly after.

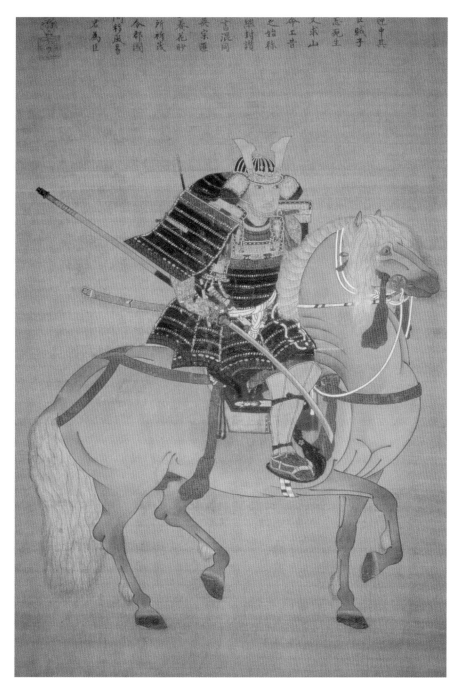

## Hosokawa Tadaoki
### (1564–1645)
### Tokugawa era *daimyo*

Hosokawa Tadaoki was an early Tokugawa era *daimyo* of Nakatsu and Kokura domains, and an important military commander. His father was the noted scholar and poet Hosokawa Fujitaka, an adviser to Ashikaga Yoshiaki and Oda Nobunaga. At the age of fifteen, Tadaoki fought in his first battle alongside his father. and afterward they were gifted the province of Tango. Tadaoki went on to fight for Toyotomi Hideyoshi in the Komaki Campaign and the Odawara Campaign (1590). During the 1590s he befriended Tokugawa Ieyasu; at the battle of Sekigahara in 1600 Tadaoki commanded 5,000 men in the Tokugawa vanguard. He was awarded the Kokura fief in Buzen and went on to serve in the sieges of Osaka (1614 and 1615). In 1632 he received a huge fief in Higo. A noted warrior and also a learned scholar, Tadaoki was also rather an ill-tempered man. He had frequently quarreled with his father and apparently made a habit of killing his servants.

**Left:** Hosokawa Sumimoto was declared *kanrei* and inherited all of the Hosokawa's holdings on Shikoku. *Sakamoto Photo Research Laboratory/Corbis*

**Far left:** Three warriors on the field of battle. *via Clive Sinclaire*

# Ichijo Kanesada
## (1543–1585)
**Sengoku era *daimyo***

Ichijo Kanesada was a late Sengoku era *daimyo* in Tosa Province, who earned an enduring reputation for great brutality during his lifetime. Kanesada was the son of Fusamoto, the fourth head of the Ichijo clan of regents. He was a deeply unpopular figure among his retainers, prompting many to abandon him. Among them was Chosokabe Motochika, who rose up against Kanesada and took Tosa Province, driving Kanesada into exile in Kyushu (Bungo) in 1574.

Otomo Sorin, who was Kanesada's nephew, subsequently sent Kanesada to Kojima Island (Iyo Province). Motochika took over Iyo shortly following this event, and may have played a hand in Kanesada's death in 1585.

**Below:** Ichijo Kanesada (on the left), was head of the Ichijo clan, from Tosa Province in the Sengku era. Kanesada was regarded as a cruel leader and faced an uprising by a number of his important retainers. Some of the numerous stories of his viciousness were undoubtedly propaganda put about by his many enemies. *British Museum/Jo St Mart*

# Ii Naomasa
## (1561–1602)
### Sengoku era general

Ii Naomasa was a late Sengoku era general under Tokugawa Ieyasu, and one of the legendary "Four Guardians" of the Tokugawa. He was the only son of Ii Naochika, an Imagawa vassal, and first rose to prominence during the Komaki Campaign, notably at the battle of Nagakute in 1584, where he led a detachment of *harquebusiers* with distinction.

In 1600 at the battle of Sekigahara, Naomasa commanded a division of cavalry that opened the fighting. During the dying moments of this battle Naomasa was wounded by a stray bullet, suffering a wound that incapacitated him during later life. Resplendent in blood red armor (a style he adopted from Yamagata Masakage), Ii and the unit of cavalry he commanded cut a distinctive profile on the battlefield, and came to be known as the "Red Devils." Naomasa was held in high regard by Tokugawa Ieyasu, but finally succumbed to the effects of his injuries in 1602.

**Right:** Ii Naomasa was famous for sending his ferocious men into battle wearing red armor, which led to their nickname "Red Devils." He was himself sometimes known as *Akaoni*—meaning Red Devil. This statue of him is in Hikone in Shiga, Japan. *British Museum/Jo St Mart*

## Ikeda Nobuteru
### (1536–1584)
### Sengoku and Azuchi-Momoyama period *daimyo* and military commander

Nobuteru was a *daimyo* and military commander during the Sengoku period and Azuchi-Momoyama period, and an important military commander in the service of both Oda Nobunaga and later Toyotomi Hideyoshi. In 1560, at the age of only fourteen, Nobuteru had his first command, and was present at the defeat of Imagawa Yoshimoto at Okehazama in June of that same year. In 1566 he received Kinota castle in Mino province, and in 1570 took part in Nobunaga's campaign against the Azai and Asakura in Omi.

Following their decisive defeat in the battle of Anegawa, Nobuteru was made castellan of Inuyama castle. He also commanded troops at the battle of Nagashino in 1575 and in 1580 was given Osaka castle. Following Nobunaga's death in June 1582, Nobuteru hastened to join Toyotomi Hideyoshi and fought at Yamazaki. He also supported Hideyoshi in the defeat of Shibata Katsuie in 1583, and for this was given Ogaki castle in Mino; his two eldest sons Yukisuke and Terumasa held Gifu and Ikejiri respectively. In 1584 the Ikeda house joined Hideyoshi's campaign against Tokugawa Ieyasu and was dispatched to confront him at Mikawa. However, Nobuteru's army was attacked at Nagakute by Tokugawa troops and in

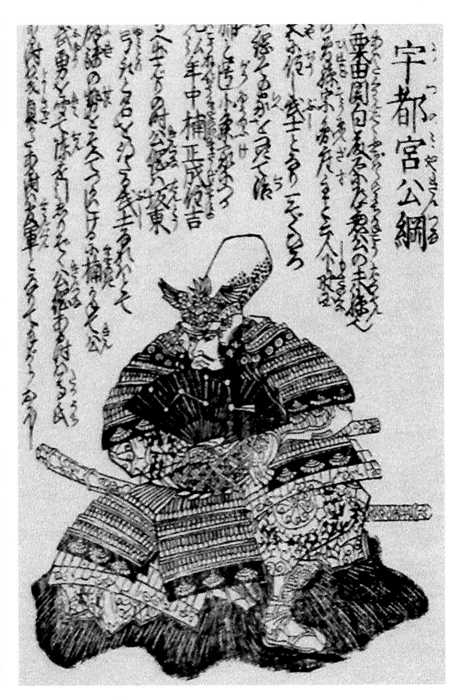

the course of the fighting Nobuteru received a fatal spear wound.

Soon afterwards, Nobuteru's son Yukisuke was also killed. Hideyoshi was said to have grieved at Nobuteru's death; he wrote a letter of condolence to Nobuteru's widow, saying "There is simply nothing I can say about the recent [death of your husband] Shonyu and your son. I share your sorrow and your grief . . . Numberless times I convey my anguish."

**Left:** Ikeda Nobuterua first faced battle at fourteen and later became a *daimyo* and retainer of the notorious warlord Oda Nobunaga, then after his death of Toyotomi Hideyoshi. *British Museum/Jo St Mart*

**Above:** A detail from a panel showing the siege of Osaka castle, November 1614–January 1615. © *Werner Forman/Corbis*

## Imagawa Yoshimoto
### (1519–1560)
### Sengoku era *daimyo*

Imagawa Yoshimoto was an early Sengoku era *daimyo*, with a power-base centered in Suruga Province. His clan was one of the dominant powers in the Tokaido region until his death in 1560.

Yoshimoto was a third son of Imagawa Ujichika, and spent much of his early life in a monastery, seemingly destined for the Buddhist clergy. However, at the age of twenty-five he became the focus of a succession dispute over who would succeed his brother Ujichika as leader of the clan. The Imagawa split into two factions, one favoring Yoshomoto, and the other his elder half brother, Genko Etan. Yoshimoto defeated and killed his rival during the Hanakura no ran. He subsequently made efforts to influence the Takeda clan in neighboring Kai Province, and was instrumental in Takeda Shingen's *coup d'état* in 1540. Yoshimoto now began a westward expansion, which brought him into conflict with the Oda clan in Mikawa, fighting with them on a number of occasions.

In 1544, Yoshimoto, in alliance with the Takeda, marched on the Hojo. Little was achieved and he reached a peaceful accord after a battle at Kitsunebashi. By the late 1550s he had wrested control of a wide area including Suruga, Totomi, and Mikawa, and felt secure enough to face off the challenge of the upstart Oda Nobunaga. In June 1560 he moved on Kyoto, but was surprised and heavily defeated at Okezahama. Yoshimoto himself was slain, and thereafter the Imagawa lost their power and influence, eventually becoming retainers of the Tokugawa clan.

**Above:** Imagawa Yoshimoto in battle. *via Clive Sinclaire*

**Left:** Imagawa Yoshimoto is said to have shaved his eyebrows and blackened his teeth in the fashion of a Kyoto noble. *British Museum/Jo St Mart*

# Ishida Mitsunari
(1560–1600)
**Sengoku/Azuchi-Momoyama era *daimyo* and general**

Ishida Mitsunari was a late Sengoku/Azuchi-Momoyama era *daimyo* and general. Although first and foremost a bureaucrat, he is however best known as the commander of the "Western" Army at the battle of Sekigahara in 1600. Mitsunari was the second son of Ishida Masatsugu, a retainer for the Azai in Omi Province. Following the defeat and death of Asai Nagamasa at Odani in 1573, the Ishida withdrew their support. In around 1578, Ishida Mitsunari was taken into the service of Toyotomi Hideyoshi, chiefly because of his keen administrative skills, and demonstrated a talent for finance. From 1585, together with his brother Masazumi, he was administrator of Sakai Province. Later Hideyoshi made him the *daimyo* of Sawayama in Omi.

Mistrusted by Hideyoshi's military for his unmilitary bearing and scheming, he went to Korea during the second campaign on the continent and there engendered the hatred of Kuroda Yoshitaka and Kobayakawa Hideaki. After Hideyoshi's death, Mitsunari was appointed as one the five regents charged with governing until Hideyoshi's son came of age. His already strained relationship with Tokugawa Ieyasu became openly hostile and the regents divided into two competing factions. The outcome of this was the battle of Sekigahara in 1600, fought between the Western Army of Ishida Mitsunari, Mori Terumoto, Uesugi Kagekatsu, and Ukita Hidiie, and the Eastern forces of Tokugawa Ieyasu and Maeda Toshinaga. Tokugawa Ieyasu won the day, and Mitsunari fled the field. He was caught near the battlefield and transported to Kyoto, where he was executed by beheading in November. After the execution, his head was displayed in public for all to see.

**Left:** Ishida Mitsunari fought at the battle of Sekigahara and organized an army led by Mori Termumoto but a coalition led by Tokugawa Ieyasu overwhelmed him. After his defeat he was caught by villagers and was beheaded in Kyoto. *British Museum/Jo St Mart*

## Kajiwara Kagetoki
### (c. 1162–1200)
#### Genpei War military commander

Kajiwara Kagetoki was a military commander under Minamoto no Yoritomo during the Genpei War. He was born in Suruga province, and rose to become the governor of neighboring Sagami province. Kajiwara began the Genpei War in the military service of Oba Kagechika, one of the Taira generals. After the Taira victory at Ishibashiyama in 1181, he pursued Yoritomo into the Hakone Mountains, but was then persuaded to change allegiance to the Minamoto cause.

By 1184 Kajiwara was one of Yoritomo's most valued allies and fought several battles against the Taira, culminating in Ichi-no-tani. However, his true role within the command structure was to monitor Yoshitsune and report what he saw and heard to Yoritomo. A mutual dislike was quickly fostered, amplified by disagreements over strategy and Kagetoki's grievance over a purported slur he was dealt by Yoshitsune.

Kagetoki exploited the mistrust between Yoshinaka and his brother, leading Yoritomo to accuse Yoshitsune of fomenting a plot against him. The consequences of this were

**Left:** Kajiwara Kagetoki was a military commander notorious for his greed and treachery and even worked as a spy in the Genpei War. He was continuously embroiled in devious plots, especially at court, to discredit his enemies. *British Museum/Jo St Mart*

**Above:** Kajiwara Kagetoki and and Minamoto Yoshitsune in battle. *via Clive Sinclaire*

severe; Yoshitsune was banished and a unbridgeable rift opened opened between the brothers, leading to war in 1189. This and other instances of Kajiwara's ceaseless machinating at court made him many enemies, and the enduring image of the man is negative. Eventually, his scheming proved to be his undoing. In 1199, he named Yuki Tomomitsu as the instigator of a plot against *shogun* Minamoto no Yoriie. A group of courtiers pressed for his removal and he fled Kamakura

for Suruga. The following year he was defeated and killed in battle along with his son Kagesue.

## Kato Kiyomasa
### (1562–1611)
### Sengoku and early Edo era *daimyo*

Kato Kiyomasa was a *daimyo* of the late Sengoku and early Edo period. In the service of Toyotomi Hideyoshi he distinguished himself on a number of occasions and was one of the group of generals known as the *Shizugatake no shichi-hon-yari* or Seven Spears of

Shizugatake. Although military matters dominated his life, there was another side to his legendary toughness. Like many samurai, he was a follower of the *Nichiren Shu* Buddhist sect, and encouraged the building of Nichiren temples.

Kiyomasa was born in Owari Province to Kato Kiyotada, who died when Kiyomasa was young boy. Soon after, Kiyomasa (known in his youth as Toranosuke) entered service with Hideyoshi. He fought in Hideyoshi's army at the battle of Yamazaki, and later at the battle of Shizugatake. For his bravery and leadership in this last battle he garnered entry to the elite Seven Spears of Shizugatake, and the reward of lands worth 3,000 koku.

After Hideyoshi became the *kampaku* in the summer of 1585, Kiyomasa was at court. In 1586 he was given extensive lands in Higo Province and Kumamoto castle as his provincial residence.

In 1592, Hideyoshi selected him as one of the three commanders of the expedition to the continent. Together with Konishi Yukinaga, he captured Seoul, fighting so fiercely that the Koreans named him "Devil Kiyomasa." Japanese books will tell you that the Korean king Seonjo abandoned his family and deserted Seoul in fear of Kiyomasa. His most famous actions of the Korean campaigns was at Ulsan in 1598, which he twice defended against relentless attacks from the Chinese army.

Kiyomasa was undoubtedly a tough, uncompromising man, whose life was shaped by war. He was also intolerant of weakness in others. During the first campaign, Konishi Yukinaga's concessions to the Chinese during truce negotiations angered both Toyotomi and Kiyomasa, leading the latter to attack and ravage the Konishi domain in Higo in retribution.

When alliances were forged in lead up to the battle of Sekigahara, Kiyomasa threw in his lot sided with Tokugawa Ieyasu, and after his victory Kiyomasa was given territories that had belonged to his old enemy Konishi (who had sided with Ishida). In his later years, Kiyomasa had the difficult role of mediator between Ieyasu and Toyotomi Hideyori. He was engaged on a mission to Kumamoto in 1611 when he suddenly died.

**Left:** Kimura Mataso fighting another samurai, while Kato Kiyomasa watches on from his horse. *via Clive Sinclaire*

**Following page:** Two more depictions of Kato Kiyomasa in action. *via Clive Sinclaire*

# Kato Yoshiaki
**(1563–1631)**
**Sengoku and early Edo era**
*daimyo*

Kato Yoshiaki was a late Sengoku and early Edo era *daimyo*, retainer to Oda Nobunaga, Toyotomi Hideyoshi, and Tokugawa Ieyasu and one of the *shichi-hon-yari* or Seven Spears of Shizugatake.

Like the other members of this elite, Yoshiaki had distinguished himself fighting for Toyotomi Hideyoshi at the battle of Shizugatake in 1583. He was also an accomplished naval commander, a role in which he served in Toyotomi's campaigns in Kyushu and Odawara, and was later rewarded with land in Ise Province. During the Korean campaigns he was recalled from duties on land to counter the pressing threat of the Korean navy under Yi Sun-sin, but was defeated at Hansando in August 1592.

Following the death of Hideyoshi in 1598 Yoshiaki aligned himself with Tokugawa Ieyasu and led 3,000 men at Sekigahara. Beginning in 1603, he started on the construction of Matsuyama castle, and saw it completed twenty-five years later when he was sixty-five years old. He lived until 1631.

**Right:** Kato Yoshiaki was one of the *Shizugatake no shichi-hon-yari* or Seven Spears of Shizugatake.
*British Museum/Jo St Mart*

71

## Kiso Yoshimasa
(1540–1595)
Takeda clan retainer

**Above:** Kiso Yoshimasa (standing) was the warlord over Shinano Province who failed to prevent Takeda Shingen from expanding into his province. *British Museum/Jo St Mart*

## Kitabatake Akiie
(1318–1338)
Influential court noble

Kiso Yoshimasa was an important retainer of the Takeda clan during the part of the Sengoku period. Although his father, the Kiso clan leader Yoshiyasu, had actively opposed Takeda Shingen's attempts to expand into Shinano. Yoshimasa served as a retainer under the Takeda clan but after Shingen's death and the decline of the clan under Katsuyori,

Yoshimasa joined Oda Nobunaga. Katsuyori sent an army to try and bring Yoshimasa back into line but this failed. Following his defection he was generously rewarded by Nobunaga. Subsequent to Nobunaga's death in 1582, Yoshimasa served Toyotomi Hideyoshi. Yoshimasa died in 1595.

Kitabatake Akiie was a court noble, and one of Emperor Go-Daigo's most important allies during the *Namboku-cho* Wars. He was also *chinjufu shogu* (commander-in-chief of the defense of the north), and governor of Mutsu Province. In 1334, when he was just sixteen years old, Akiie was appointed Governor of Mutsu (which included modern Aomori, Iwate, Miyagi, and

Fukushima Prefectures) at the time of the Kemmu Restoration However, the role was purely titular, for his actual duty was to bring peace to the areas of Mutsu and Dewa, which constituted the northeastern area of Honshu. This remote, hostile area was notoriously unstable, and at first, Akiie needed some inducement to accept the appointment. Soon afterward, he was appointed to the post of *chinjufu shogun*, or commander-in-chief of the defense of the north.

Akiie led a faction that included many of the powerful northern clans, including Yuki, Date, Nambu, Soma, and Tamura, in support of Go-Daigo when he established his breakaway Southern Court. During the early years of the *Namboku-cho jidai*, Akiie fought Ashikaga Takauji in Kyoto. Go-Daigo demanded that Akiie bring his army south to counter a renewed push on the capital by the Northern Court. During the march south he won a battle at Tonegawa, in December before taking the shogunate capital, Kamakura. From here he moved on Nara, fighting at Iga and Sekigahara, but was driven back to Kawachi. He regrouped but in April 1338 was again defeated at Tenno-ji in Settsu (near modern-day Osaka). Two months later in June he was defeated and killed at Izumi in 1338, still barely twenty years old.

**Right:** Kitabatake Akiie was a court noble who supported the Southern Court during the *Nanboku-cho* Wars. He died at the age of twenty, after having fought and won many battles. *British Museum/Jo St Mart*

# Kiyohara no Iehira
## (d.1087)
### Ambitious Kiyohara clan member

Kiyohara no Iehira was a member of the Kiyohara, a powerful clan in the far northern Tohoku region of Honshu during the Heian Period, and linear descendants of Emperor Temmu (631–686). The Gosannen War was a direct consequence of conflict between Iehira and his brothers Narihira and Masahira.

After the Zenkunnen War the Kiyohara took over the administration of Mutsu, along with Dewa. However, over the next two decades the three branches of the family, headed by Iehira, Narihira, and Masahira, became deeply divided over differences arising from intermarriage with different warrior families. Each believed he should head the main family line. In 1083, this conflict erupted into outright violence, and Minamoto no Yoshiie was dispatched to the region to restore order. Yoshiie allied himself to Iehira, and made attempts to reach a resolution with the others. When that failed, Yoshiie and Iehira (and Fujiwara no Kiyohira), attacked and defeated Kiyohara no Sanehira.

Now however, a rift developed

**Right:** Kiyohara no Iehira was a member of the Kiyohara clan, which wielded significant power in the Thoku region from around 1063 to 1089, during the Heian period. He was also a key participant in the Gosannen War which grew out of conflicts within the clan. *British Museum/Jo St Mart*

between Yoshiie and Iehira as the latter sought to fulfill his own ambitions. Over the course of three years Yoshiie made a series of assaults on Kanezawa fortress; and in 1087 finally succeeded in taking it. Both Iehira and his uncle, Kiyohara no Tahahira died in the action.

## Kobayakawa Hideaki
### (1577–1602)
### Nephew of Toyotomi Hideyoshi

The nephew of Toyotomi Hideyoshi, he was adopted by Kobayakawa Takakage, who died in 1596 leaving him well off. Hideaki will be remembered as the man whose changing sides during the battle of Sekigahara tipped the balance against Mitsunari. He did so because of an enmity that went back to the Second Korean Campaign in the late 1590s. Mitsunari had criticized Hideaki, and Hideyoshi had demoted him accordingly, moving him to a lesser fief. Hideaki would never forgive Mitsunari and his chance came on October 21, 1600. After Sekigahara Hideaki pursued his erstwhile allies but died suddenly two years later.

**Right:** A ghost appearing to Kobayakawa Hideaki—here under the name Kingo Chunagon Hideaki. *Asian Art & Archaeology, Inc./Corbis*

**Left:** As head of the Kobayakawa clan, Kobayakawa Takakage expanded the clan's territory in the Chugoku region (now Western Honshu), and fought for the Mori clan throughout their campaigns. After later swearing loyalty and arms to Hideyoshi, he was rewarded with lands in Iyo Province on Shikoku and Chikuzen Province on Kyushu. *British Museum/Jo St Mart*

# Kobayakawa Takakage
## (1533–1597)
### Sengoku era *daimyo*

Kobayakawa Takakage was a Sengoku era *daimyo* in the Chugoku region, and retainer of Toyotomi Hideyoshi. Takakage was the son of the prominent *daimyo* Mori Motonari, but was adopted by the head of the Kobayakawa clan, Takakage, took his name, and succeeded his adoptive father to become head of the clan following his death in 1545.

Under Takakage's stewardship the clan's territory was expanded in the Chugoku region of western Honshu, and he lent his support to his legiti-mate family by in their military campaigns. Initially, he opposed both Oda Nobunaga and Toyotomi Hideyoshi, but later took up with Hideyoshi. In his service Takakage took part in Hideyoshi's invasions of Shikoku, Kyushu, and Korea. He was then awarded domains in Iyo province on Shikoku and Chikuzen province on Kyushu. On his death in 1597 he was succeeded as leader of the clan by his adopted son Kobayakawa Hideaki, formerly an adopted son of Hideyoshi.

**Below:** Kondo Isami's exploits as a samurai and Shinsengumi commander have made him a great hero of Japanese culture in books, television, and movies. *British Museum/Jo St Mart*

# Kondo Isami
## (1834–1868)
### Commander of the *Shinsengumi*

Kondo Isami was an official of the *shogunate* during the late Edo period, best known as commander of the *Shinsengumi* (literally "group of new chosen ones"). His family were humble farmers from Tama (now in Tokyo). In 1863 Kondo, joined the *roshigumi* in Edo, before it transferred to Kyoto. The *roshigumi* was a group of masterless samurai or *ronin* whose ostensible task it was to protect the emperor. When the group was dissolved by its founder, Kiyokawa Hachiro, many members, including

Kondo, remained in Kyoto. There they formed the *miburo roshigumi*, which effectively was the police force in the capital under the control of the pro-Tokugawa Aizu clan. Kondo had originally been one of three *kyoku-chou* commanders (with Niimi Niishiki and Serizawa Kamo), but their deaths left Kondou as the sole leader. Under the leadership of Kondo, the rough, ill-disciplined and violent *shinsengumi* improved its reputation as a source for law and order.

Kondo was still in command when the Tokugawa *bakufu* finally collapsed. He continued to fight for the shogunate in the Boshin War, but was beaten at the battle of Toba-Fushimi in January and after at Koshu-Katsunuma and was finally captured at Nagareyama. Although he had lived as a samurai, he was denied the right of *seppuku* because of his lowly birth. In May 1868 he was beheaded in Kyoto, and his head put on public display.

**Right:** Early photograph of two Edo policemen. *via Clive Sinclaire*

**Far right:** Most unusually Konishi Yukinaga was a devout Christian (in which capacity he was known as Dom Agostinho) and consequently would not commit *seppuku* after being defeated at the battle of Sekigahara (1600). He was executed by his enemies instead. *British Museum/Jo St Mart*

forces into Korea. During that first campaign he distinguished himself in the capture of Busan and Seoul and the defense of Pyongyang. However, he incurred the wrath of both Hideyoshi and Kato Kiyomasa through his handling of negotiations with the Chinese. Despite garnering accusations of disloyalty, Yukinaga weathered the storm and was selected as one of a triumvirate commanders for the second invasion of Korea.

After Hideyoshi's death, Yukinaga sided with Ishida Mitsunari's coalition. Following the defeat at Sekigahara, he fled to Mount Ibuki, but was captured by Takenaka Shigekado's forces. As a Christian, Yukinaga refused *seppuku* and was executed instead.

## Kuki Yoshitaka
**(1542–1600)**
**Father of the Japanese navy**

Kuki Yoshitaka was a naval commander during the Sengoku era under Oda Nobunaga and later, Toyotomi Hideyoshi. He was head of Toba castle and admiral of the *Kumano Suigun* Navy, and generally regarded as founder of the Japanese Navy. The family into which Yoshitaka was born in 1542 had held the positions of *Kumano Betto* and *Kumano Sanzan Kengyo* from the time of Go-Shirakawa, and were thus well versed in naval matters.

After a period of service under the provincial administrator of Ise province, in the 1570s, Yoshitaka commanded Oda Nobunaga's fleet in

## Konishi Yukinaga
**(1555–1600)**
**Sengoku era *daimyo***

Konishi Yukinaga was a late Sengoku era *daimyo* under Toyotomi Hideyoshi. He was probably born in Sakai, located in the Chubu region, and was first in the service of the Ukita of Bizen Province. He met

Toyotomi Hideyoshi during the latter's Chugoku Campaign (1577–1582) while acting as an Ukita negotiator. Hideyoshi was impressed with Yukinaga and convinced him to join his own forces. In 1587, during the Invasion of Kyushu, he quelled the local uprising in Higo province and was awarded a fief in that province.

By 1592 Yukinaga had risen high within the command structure and was charged with leading the first

the attack on Oshima castle (1574) and also during the reduction of the *Ikko-ikki* fortress at Nagashima from his famous flagship *Nipponmaru*. In 1576, he lost the first action at the first battle of Kizugawaguchi to a "Mÿri clan" Mori fleet, but emerged as victor at the second battle of Kizugawaguchi battle two years later. It is recorded that in this action he used several *atakebune* (iron ships), which were reportedly impregnable to arrows and musket balls.

For his help in the battle against the Mori, Yoshitaka received land in Shima and Ise provinces, and then built his castle at Toba. After the death of Nobunaga he became a vassal of Toyotomi Hideyoshi, and in 1587, was one of Hideyoshi's naval commanders during the campaign in Kyushu. In 1590, with Wakizaka Yasuharu and Kato Yoshiaki, he led the sieges of Odawara and Shimoda. He continued in his role as commander of Hideyoshi's fleet during the first invasion of Korea in 1592. However, he was conspicuously defeated at Hansando in August by the Korean admiral Yi Sun-sin.

In the battle of Sekigahara, Yoshitaka fought alongside the Toyotomi forces, while his son Moritaka joined the opposing force, under Tokugawa Ieyasu. On November 17, 1600, he committed suicide, unaware that he had been pardoned.

**Right:** Kuki Yoshitaka came from a family of warlord pirates and was associated with maritime warfare all his life, including two invasions of Korea. *British Museum/Jo St Mart*

# Kuroda Nagamasa
## (1568–1623)
### *Daimyo* and general during late Sengoku and early Edo periods

Kuroda Nagamasa was a *daimyo* during the late Sengoku and early Edo period, and an important general under Oda Nobunaga, Toyotomi Hideyoshi, Tokugawa Ieyasu, and finally Tokugawa Hidetada.

Nagamasa was born in 1568 in Harima Province, the son of Kuroda Yoshitaka. In 1576, when Nagamasa was a child of only eight, Yoshitaka sent him to Oda Nobunaga as a material guarantee of his loyalty. Nobunaga sent him to live at Nagahama castle in Omi Province, and then took him into service. During a diplomatic mission for Nobunaga to Itami castle Nagamasa was held hostage again, and his absence was interpreted as a sign of disloyalty. Nobunaga accordingly ordered that the young Nagamasa be executed at once, an order that fortuitously was never carried out.

Following Nobunaga's assassination in 1582, the Kuroda enjoyed further good fortunes, facilitated by

**Above:** Kuroda Nagamasa beating Watanabe Shinnojio during the battle of Sekigahara on October 21, 1600. The result of victory was to allow Tokugawa Ieyasu to become *shogun. via Clive Sinclaire*

Yoshitaka's cordial relationship with Toyotomi Hideyoshi. During the 1587 invasion of Kyushu Nagamasa distinguished himself in at Takarabe castle, and for his actions was given lands in Buzen Province valued at around 50,000 *koku*. In the year of his twenty-first birthday, Nagamasa was awarded the title "Kai no kami" and succeeded his father as clan leader.

## Kuroda Yoshitaka
(1546–1604)
*Daimyo,* general and strategist during the late Sengoku/early Edo period

Kuroda Yoshitaka was a *daimyo* and general of the late Sengoku through early Edo periods, who achieved distinction as chief strategist under Toyotomi Hideyoshi.

Yoshitaka was the son of Kuroda Mototaka, one of the chief retainers of the Odera clan and the holder of Himeji castle. In 1567, at the age of twenty-one, Yoshitaka succeeded his father as head of the clan. Some years later during Oda Nobunaga's campaign against the Mori clan in the Chugoku region, Yoshitaka lent critical support to Hideyoshi and Akechi Mitsuhide, enabling them to isolate the Ishiyama Honganji and gain access to Bizen and "new" Mimasaka.

Yoshitaka became a trusted friend of Hideyoshi, who regarded him almost like a brother. He campaigned for Hideyoshi on Shikoku in 1585 and two years later in Kyushu, for which he received a sizable fief in "new" Buzon. During the Second Korean Campaign Yoshitaka was chief advisor to the commander-in-chief, Kobayakawa Hideaki. While in Korea he clashed with Ishida Mitsunari when the latter charged him with

Three years Nagamasa led 6,000 men onto the Korean peninsula, and six years later held the shrinking bridgehead at Pusan during the withdrawal. For his service in Korea he was given a substantial fief at Nakatsu in Buzen.

In Korea Nagamasa distinguished himself in the action at Pusan, during the general withdrawal of Japanese forces. For his service during the campaigns he was given substantial *han* at Nakatsu in Buzen.

Subsequently, both Nagamasa and his father rallied to Tokugawa Ieyasu's cause against Ishida Mitsunari. At Sekigahara, Nagamasa's

**Above:** Kuroda Nagamasa kneels at a temple to pray before the decisive battle of Sekigahara. From this time on the Tokugawa *bakufu* became the last shogunate to control Japan. *British Museum/Jo St Mart*

5,400 men in the Tokugawa van earned the plaudits of Tokugawa Ieyasu; in the aftermath of the Tokugawa victory, Nagamasa was given a huge fief in at Najima in Chikuzen province. Fukuoka castle is part of his legacy to that area. He served in the Osaka castle campaigns and fought under Tokugawa Hidetada. In 1623 Nagamasa fell ill in Kyoto and died at the Chionji temple.

**Right:** Kuroda Yoshitaka was a *daimyo* of the late Sengoku Period through to the early Edo Period. He was the chief strategist under Toyotomi Hideyoshi. *British Museum/Jo St Mart*

mishandling the war, resulting in Yoshitaka's recall.

Following Hideyoshi's death in 1598, this and other slurs by Ishida caused Yoshitaka to declare for Tokugawa Ieyasu. In the months before the battle of Sekigahara, Yoshitaka assembled a force to fight on Kyushu and in union with Kato Kiyomasa took a number of pro-Ishida castles in "new" Bungo and "new" Chikuzen. They were on the cusp of invading the Shimazu lands in Satsuma, Osumi, and Hyuga provinces when the defeat of the Ishida coalition at Sekigahara brought the war to a sudden end.

It's interesting to note that Yoshitaka was one of a large number of Christian *daimyo*, and was baptized with the name Dom Simeão. He used his influence to gain clemency for Otomo Sorin (also a Christian) and, in 1584, expedited the rescue of a Jesuit mission in Bungo when the Shimazu clan invaded the province.

**Right:** Two views of Himeji castle at the base of Mount Himeji. Originally started in 1331 the castle was extended and fortified over the years. In the late sixteenth century Kuroda Yoshitaka built a three-story tower, then in other hands, the castle expanded for a further forty or so years until it reached its current extent. *fotoLibra*

# Kusunoki Masahige

(1294–1336)
**Kamakura period military commander**

Kusunoki Masashige was a military commander during the Kamakura period, and the most important of Emperor Go-Daigo's allies in his attempt to bring down the Kamakura Shogunate. Masashige's devoted service to the emperor and the imperial cause were heralded for centuries after his death.

Although little is known about him prior to his enrollment in the imperial forces by Go-Daigo, the Taiheiki says that Kusunoki were descendants of emperor Bidatsu, but living by choice "among the common people of Kawachi province." Emperor Godaigo summoned Masahige, and appointed him to the imperial forces.

Masahige rose to become a respected, if unorthodox, commander (he often had recourse to sneak attacks) yet through his defense of the key loyalist fortresses at Chihayaakasaka, Osaka Akasaka and Chihaya, Go-Daigo was briefly able to return to power. Soon however, the imperial faction was compromised by the duplicity of Ashikaga Takauji, and Masahige advised the Emperor to abandon Kyoto. He refused and Masahige reluctantly marched out to confront Takauji's army at the battle of Minatogawa in modern-day Chuoku, (aka Kobe). The battle was a rout and Masahige, his army completely surrounded, committed suicide along with 600 of his surviving troops. According to legend, his last words were *"shichisei hokoku!"* ("Would that I had seven lives to give for my country!")

In later years Kusunoki's name was resurrected and he was enshrined as a patriotic hero, the personification of loyalty, courage, and devotion to the emperor.

**Below:** Arrows fill the air during the battle of Shijo Nawate in 1348. The fight was between the Southern army led by Kusunoki Masatsura and the Northern army fighting for the Northern emperor. The latter prevailed and Kusunoki committed *seppuku. via Clive Sinclaire*

**Right:** Kusunoki Masashige and his brother Masasue committed *seppuku* after being routed at the battle of Minatogawa (present day Kobe). They were also joined by those Kusunoki retainers who had not already been killed. Masashige's last words were reported to be, *Shichisei hokoku!* ("Would that I had seven lives to give for my country!). *via Clive Sinclaire*

**Below right:** Kusunoki Masashige prepares to fight for the emperor. Behind him, his helmet and standard bearers attend him. *via Clive Sinclaire*

**Left:** A magnificent suit of samurai armor from Himeji castle. *fotolibra*

**Left:** In his early life a modest landowner from Kawachi province, Kusunoki Masashige become an inspiring symbol of loyalty to the emperor and a hero in Meiji era legends. *British Museum/Jo St Mart*

**Below:** The escape of Emperor Go-Daigo (the 96th emperor of Japan) from the Oki Islands in 1333, during the event known as the Genko Incident. *via Clive Sinclaire*

## Kusunoki Masatsura
### (1326–1348)
### Southern Court military commander

Kusunoki Masatsura was a military commander in the service of the Southern Court during the *Namboku cho jidai*. His father was the legendary Kusunoki Masashige, a staunch supporter of Go-Daigo during the Nambokucho jidai. Masatsura was an accomplished strategist and through his efforts the Southern Court began to make up for the stagnation that had blighted earlier efforts. In 1347, Masatsura led an attack on *bakufu* loyalists in Kii Province, winning fresh support from Kii, as well as Izumi and Settsu Provinces. That same year shogun Ashikaga Takauji dispatched a force led by Hosokawa Akiuji to confront Masatsura, but Masatsura defeated this at the battle of Sakainoura.

He fought several more campaigns against the bakufu, and was personally praised for the loyalty of his family by Go-Murakami. On February 4, 1348, at the age of 22, Masatsura was killed at the battle of Shijo Nawate.

# Meada Toshiie
## (1539–1599)
### Sengoku/early Azuchi-Momoyama Period *daimyo*

Maeda Toshiie was *daimyo* of one of the most powerful samurai families and a leading general in one of Oda Nobunaga's service during the late Sengoku Period and early Azuchi-Momoyama Period. He was born at Arako castle in Owari Province, the fourth of Maeda Toshimasa's seven sons, and in his childhood was affectionately known as "Inuchiyo."

He entered Oda Nobunaga's service in 1551 as a page. Toshiie was rather a wild youth, following the style of a *kabukimono* (crazy one) and in his youth befriended the young Toyotomi Hideyoshi. Unusually, since he had three elder brothers, Toshiie succeeded as head of the clan. Toshiie was rather a wild youth, following the style of a *kabukimono* (crazy one). In his youth he befriended one Kinoshita Tokichiro (later Toyotomi Hideyoshi) in their youth.

Toshiie began his military career as a member of the unit under Oda Nobunaga's personal command. He later became an infantry captain (*ashigaru taisho*) in the Oda army. It seems that at some time he fell out of favor with Nobunaga supposedly for killing another of his retainers, but after fighting in the battles at Okehazama (1560) and Moribe (1561), he was recognized as a retainer. He later fought at Anegawa (1570) and Nagashino (1570) and was given a fief in Echizen Province in 1575, thus becoming one of the so-called *Echizen sanninshu*.

After 1576 Toshiie assisted Shibata Katsuie in his push north into Kaga province. At this time Kaga was under the control of the Ikko-ikki, and who proved to particularly resilient opponents. After 1577 Toshiie battled with the Uesugi of Echigo who were openly hostile to Nobunaga, and also assisted in the attacks on the Toyama and Uzu in Etchu Province. For his services in 1581 he was granted a small, but valuable *han* encompassing much of Noto Province and Kaga Province.

After Nobunaga's assassination in 1582, Toshiie fought Toyotomi Hideyoshi under Katsuie's command in the battle of Shizugatake. However, subsequent to Katsuie's defeat, Toshiie was accepted into Hideyoshi's service and went on to become one of his leading generals. In 1584 he defeated his

**Above:** Maeda Toshiie was utterly loyal to Toyotomi Hideyoshi and was named as one of the five regents—the council of Five Elders—responsible for keeping the realm in order while Toyotomi Hideyori came of age. Additionally, Maeda was also named as Hideyori's guardian, but he died within a year. *British Museum/Jo St Mart*

**Far left:** Kusunoki Masatsura was the son of Masashige and a supporter of the Southern Imperial Court. He fought in the Nanbokucho wars, but aged only 22 he died in the battle of Shijÿ Nawate, in February 1348. Before he died, he composed a death poem: *I have a feeling I will not be returning, so among the names of those who died by the bow I inscribe my own. British Museum/Jo St Mart*

former friend Sasa Narimasa at the siege of Suemori castle.

Before dying in 1598, Hideyoshi named Toshiie to the *go-tairo* (council of five elders) that would act as governors to his son Hideyori until the boy came of age. One of the other elders was Tokugawa Ieyasu, with who he shared a life-long enmity. Although he struggled to contain Ieyasu's irresistible rise, Toshiie was himself already ailing, and died soon after in 1599.

# Minamoto Yorimasa
**(1106–1180)**
**Later Heian Period court official and poet**

Minamoto no Yorimasa was a noted court official and poet of the later Heian Period, who led the Minamoto forces at the beginning of the Genpei Wars. During a long career in the service of the Imperial house he held many posts. Although for most of his

early life he actively avoided getting involved in the disputes between the Minamoto and Taira clans, he did participate in the Hogen Rebellion in 1156. During the Heiji Rebellion of 1160, he gave tacit backing to the Taira no Kiyomori against Minamoto no Yoshitomo, who was eventually defeated. In 1179, Yorimasa had become head of the Minamoto clan.

In succession dispute that prefaced the Genpei Wars of 1180–1185, Yorimasa stood for Prince Mochihito,

one of several contenders for the Imperial Throne, and thus against Taira no Kiyomori and his faction. In May of 1180, he sent out an appeal to other Minamoto leaders, and to the many temples and monasteries that opposed Kiyomori. Yorimasa led Minamoto forces during the opening battle, at the Uji Bridge in Kyoto, where he tried unsuccessfully to defend the "Byÿdÿ-in. After the defeat at Uji, he committed suicide by *seppuku* at the Byodo-in. This is the earliest recorded instance of a samurai's suicide in the face of defeat. Legend has it that a servant cast his master's head into the Uji River so it could not be taken as a prize.

**Below left:** Gochin no Tajima—also known as Tajima the arrow-cutter—was a warrior monk who fought alongside the Minamoto clan forcesat the battle of Uji in 1180. *via Clive Sinclaire*

**Below:** Minamoto Yorimasa was a Buddhist monk, a court poet, and during his long career served eight different emperors. He also fought many battles, in particular leading the Minamoto armies and the warrior monks from Mii-dera into battle at the beginning of the Genpei War. His ritual suicide following defeat at the battle of Uji (1180) is the first recorded *seppuku* by a defeated samurai. *British Museum/Jo St Mart*

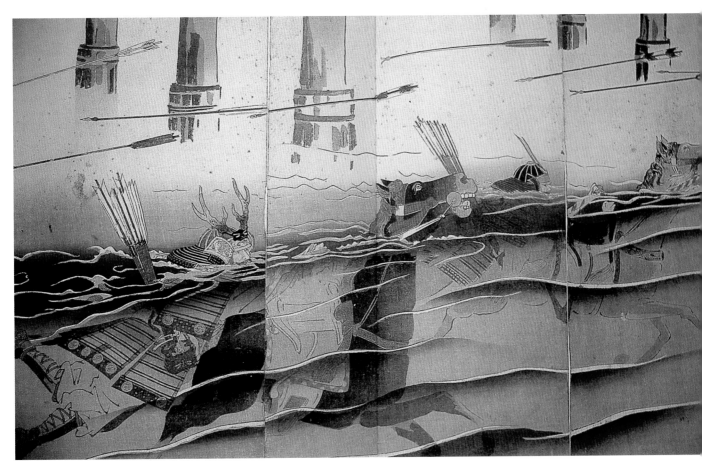

## Minamoto no Yoritomo
### (1147–1199)
### Founder and first shogun of the Kamakura shogunate

Minamoto no Yoritomo was a military commander during the Genpei Wars, and founder and first shogun of the Kamakura Shogunate of Japan from 1192 until 1199.

Yoritomo was the first son of Minamoto no Yoshitomo. While he was still just a youth of nine, the *Hogen no ran*, or "Hogen Disturbance" erupted in the capital Heian-kyo (Kyoto). The current head of the Minamoto, Tameyoshi (Yoritomo's grandfather), sided with Cloistered Emperor Sutoku while his son, Yoshitomo, formed a pact with Cloistered Emperor Toba and Emperor Go-Shirakawa. The brief civil war ended in victory for Go-Shirakawa, and his supporters Yoshitomo and Taira no Kiyomori. Tameyoshi was executed and Yoshitomo found himself elevated to the head of the Minamoto.

In the years following Yoritomo was appointed a court administrator, and soon witnessed factional disputes emerge between the Taira clan, and the Minamoto clan. In 1160,

**Left:** Portrait of Minamoto no Yoritomo. *British Museum/Jo St Mart*

**Right:** Minamoto no Yoritomo enjoying his first battle, despite the snow. *via Clive Sinclaire*

Yoshitomo and Fujiwara no Nobuyori moved to take over the capital, in the incident known as the *Heiji no ran*, or the "Heiji Disturbance." However, the coup was poorly executed and the Taira were shortly able to regain control of Kyoto.

The victorious Taira quickly vented their wrath on the Fujiwara and Minamoto forcing Yoshitomo to escape the capital for Owari Province, where he was betrayed and executed by a former retainer. His three sons, however, were spared, largely due to the intervention of Taira no Kiyomori's stepmother, Lady Ikenozenni. Yoritomo was sent into exile under the Hojo clan at Hirugashima, an island in Izu province. His half brothers, Noriyori, and Yoshitsune were sent elsewhere.

During his life in exile, Yoritomo befriended his warden, Hojo Tokimasa, and in 1179 married his daughter, Masako. When the Genpei Wars erupted in 1180, Yoritomo responded to Prince Mochihito's call to arms by raising an army. On the death of Minamoto no Yorimasa and Prince Mochihito himself at the First battle of Uji Bridge, Yoritomo set himself up as the rightful heir of the Minamoto clan, and, subsequently, with the support of the Hojo, he set up a capital at Kamakura in the east, facing off a challenge to his leadership by his uncle, Minamoto no Yukiie, and his cousin Minamoto no Yoshinaka.

In 1180, Yoritomo led an army out to confront the Taira, but was defeated at (the battle of) Ishibashiyama. Thereafter he expended much effort on winning support among the clans of the Kanto area, most of whom accepted his authority. Beginning in 1181, Taira no Munemori scaled up attacks on Minamoto bases from his Kyoto base. Yoritomo's half-brothers, Minamoto no Yoshitsune and Noriyori were sent against him, and defeated the Taira in several important battles.

Between late 1181 and 1184, there was a lull in the fighting that allowed Yoritomo to build an administration of his own, centered on Kamakura, which formed the basis for the first shogunate. However, the lingering threat presented by his cousin Yoshinaka came to a head in 1183, when Yoshinaka entered Kyoto in 1183 and enthroned a new emperor, Go-Toba. Yoritomo. In 1184 Yoritomo sent Yoshitsune and Noriyori to drive him out of the capital, leading to Yoshinaka's defeat and death at the Uji Bridge. Yoritomo now turned his full attentions on the Taira, defeating them first at Ichinotani and then decisively at the battle of Dan-no-ura in 1185.

In 1192 the first bakufu (shogunate) was formally established at Kamakura, with Yoritomo as its supreme authority. In one from or other Japan was ruled by this system until the mid-19th century. In 1199, at the age of 52, Yoritomo died unexpectedly after falling off his horse. His tomb (cenotaph) stands at the foot of a hill roughly 3,750ft northeast of Kamakura Station.

**Right:** Minamoto Yoritomo was the founder and first shogun of the Kamakura Shogunate. He had Imperial blood from his father and Fujiwara noble blood from his mother. *The Art Archive*

# Minamoto no Yoriyoshi
### (998–1082)
### Minamoto clan leader

Minamoto no Yoriyoshi was a military commander, and head of the Minamoto clan, during the Heian period.

The Minamoto were one of the four great families that dominated Japanese politics at this time. Yoriyoshi made his name commanding the Imperial government forces against the Abe family of Mutsu in the *Zenkunen kassen* (or Former Nine Years) War. He also fought some years later in the *Gosannen kassen* (Later Three Years War).

The Minanoto clan had for many years provided support to the dominant Fujiwara clan, and enjoyed their patronage. Yoriyoshi often accompanied his father Minamoto no Yorinobu on military expeditions on behalf of the Imperial Court and in 1031, went with him on just such a mission to subdue the a rebellion fomented by Taira Tadatsune. From these experiences he learnt much about the art of war. In 1051, he was commissioned to lead an expedition against the upstart Abe clan in Dewa Province, and was bestowed like his father Yorinobu, and his grandfather before that, the title of *chinjufu-shogun* (commander-in-chief of the defense of the North). The Zenkunen War would occupy him, (with brief periods of peace) for the next twelve years. In 1057 Yoriyoshi was defeated at the battle of Kawasaki by Abe Sadato, but saw the Minamoto emerge victorious five years later when his son Yoshiie beat Abe Sadato at Kuriyagawa. For his services against the Abe Yoriyoshi was awarded the governorship of Iyo Province.

**Below:** Minamoto Yoshiie, encamped near the battlefield, receives his aides. After being appointed governor of Mutsu in 1083 he put down the Kiyowara revolt in the northern provinces in the conflict known as the Later Three-Year War. *The Art Archive*

# Minamoto no Yoshiie
### (1039–1106)
### Heian Period military commander

Minamoto Yoshiie was a noted military commander in the mid-Heian period, and the man often described as the progenitor of the samurai class. As a boy of only twelve, Yoshiie went north with his father, Minamoto Yoriyoshi, on his expedition to suppress the Abe clan in Mutsu (the *Zenkunen kassen* or Former Nine-Years War), and soon proved his

talent for fighting. In 1057, when he was eighteen, he forced Abe Sadato out of his stronghold at Kawasaki, and in during the fighting retreat Yoshiie distinguished himself further. In 1062, as the war approached its conclusion, he attacked Sadato again in his fort by the Koromo River, causing him to flee to another fort by the Kuriyagawa. This was shortly brought down by Yoshiie's troops: Sadato and his son died, and his brother Muneto was captured. For his services against the Abe Yoshiie was named Governor of

源義家奥州衣川に於て貞任を追ふ

Mutsu, and was given the epithet *Hachimantaro* or Great Son of Hachiman (the God of War).

In 1083 Yoshiie, independent of the court, intervened in the affairs of a former Minamoto ally, the Kiyowara clan, which had assisted them in the preceding *Zenkunen kassen*. A power struggle had broken out in the Tohoku region among the three branches of the Kiyohara family, led by the brothers Iehira, Narihira and Masahira. Yoshiie sided with Iehira against the other two, sparking off the conflict known as the *Gosannen kassen* or Later Three-Year War. A rift developed between Yoshiie and his erstwhile ally, leading Yoshiie to launch and unsuccessful attack on Iehira's fortress at Numa in 1086. In the subsequent siege of Kanazawa, Yoshiie finally defeated the Kiyohara. Against common practice, Yoshiie received no reward of land for this service (he had received no commission from the court) and found it necessary to recompense his men from his own holdings.

By this act Yoshiie enhanced his already impressive reputation. However, although he was regarded with some awe by most courtiers, not until 1098 was he allowed to enter the Imperial court. He died ten years later in 1108.

**Above and Left:** Minamoto no Yoshiie became famous for his samurai skill and bravery. This earned him the name Hachimantaro, meaning the son of Hachiman, the god of war. *via Clive Sinclair* (above) and *British Museum/Jo St Mart* (left)

**Left:** Minamoto Yoshimitsu in battle in the Later Three-Year War of 1083–87. He is believed to be originator of the ancient Japanese martial art of *D ryu aiki-jujutsu*. This technique remained a secret w the Takeda clan until the late 19th century. *British Museum/Jo St Mart*

**Below:** Minamoto Yoshimitsu playing the flute. *v Clive Sinclaire*

# Minamoto Yoshimitsu
## (1045–1127)
### Heian Period military commander

Minamoto no Yoshimitsu was military commander during the later Heian Period, and a noted swordsman. He was the son of Minamoto no Yoriyoshi, and the brother of Minamoto no Yoshiie. He served in the *Gosannen kassen* between 1083 and 1087, fighting at the siege of Kanazawa with his brother. Thereafter he was given extensive lands in Kai, and there established the family line that in later years became the Takeda Based on his anatomical studies, Yoshimitsu developed a system of unarmed fighting that was the model for the Japanese martial art, *Daito-ryo aiki-jujutsu.*

# Minamoto Yoshinaka
## (1154–1184)
### Heian Period military commander

Minamoto no Yoshinaka was a military commander during the late Heian Period, and a key rival to Minamoto no Yoritomo during the Genpei Wars. He is one of the main characters in the Kamakura Period epic poem *Tale of Heike*. While just a young boy his father Yoshitaka was slain in an interfamily feud. The family domain was seized and the usurper, Minamoto no Yoshihira, tried to have Yoshinaka killed. Fortuitously, he was spirited away to Kiso, in Shinano Province, and brought up by the Nakahara clan.

Like his cousin Yoritomo, Yoshinaka responded toPrince Mochihito's call to arms in 1180 by raising an army in Shinano. In 1181, Yoshinaka clashed for the first time with Yoritomo when he sought to regain the family lands lost in Musashi, which was now part of Yoritomo's domain. An accord of sorts was reached, the terms of which proved to be a source of future grievance. As well as the requirement that Yoshinaka accept Yoritomo's position as the leader of the Minamoto clan, he was made to relinquish claims on his father's domain, and send his son Yoshitaka to Kanagawa as a hostage. This was undoubtedly the catalyst for future conflicts between the two cousins.

In the meantime Yoshinaka launched punitive raids against Taira lands from Shinano, and in June 1183 defeated the army of Taira no Koremori at the battle of Kurikara Pass. He then marched to Kyoto, forcing the Taira to quit the city and was given the title of Asahi *shogun* by the cloistered Emperor Go-Shirakawa. However, his relationship with Go-Shirakawa quickly deteriorated due in part to his

**Left and Right:** After winning the battle of Kurikara Pass, Yoshinaka and his army marched to Kyoto where his troops looted and burnt the city. He captured Emperor Go-Shirakawa and forced him to make him shogun, but Yoshinaka was soon driven out of Kyoto and then killed by his cousins at the battle of Awazu, in Omi Province. *via Clive Sinclaire* (left) and *British Museum/Jo St Mart* (right)

failure to carry the momentum of the campaign against the Taira. In September he finally moved out west to confront the Taira, but was defeated at the battle of Mizushima, and again at Muroyama.

Yoshinaka had by this time begun to hatch a plot to oust Go-Shirakawa. When he got wind of this the emperor sent to Yoritomo for help, but when this reached Yoshinaka's ears he extended martial law over the city, and imprisoned the Go-Shirakawa. Minamoto no Yoritomo hastily dispatched his brothers Minamoto no Yoshitsune and Noriyori south to drive Yoshinaka out of the capital.

On February 19, 1184, Yoshinaka fled Kyoto. Attempting to make a stand at the Uji Bridge, he was defeated, and forced to retreat. A few days later he was caught at Awazu, in Omi Province (present-day Shiga Prefecture), and died alongside his childhood companion Imai Kanehira.

**Below:** Tomoe Gozen was renowned for her beauty and bravery: she was the wife of Minamoto Yoshinaka and fought beside him in all his battles. *via Clive Sinclaire*

# Minamoto Yoshitomo
## (1123–1160)
### Head of the Minamoto clan

Minamoto no Yoshitomo was the head of the Minamoto clan and a noted military leader of the late Heian Period. During the *Hÿgen Rebellion* (Hogen Rebellion) in 1156, Yoshitomo lent his support to Emperor Go-Shirakawa against the faction led by retired Emperoro Sutoku and Fujiwara no Yorinaga, and which included Yoshitomo's father Minamoto no Tameyoshi.

Yoshitomo emerged truimphant from this war and became head of the Minamoto clan. In the following years he worked to establish himself and his son Yoritomo in the political hierarchy of Kyoto, but enmity between the Minamoto and Taira lingered on. In 1159 this prompted Yoshitomo and Fujiwara no Nobuyori to attempt to remove Go-Shirakawa from power. With Taira no Kiyomori absent from the capital, Go-Shirakawa was placed under house arrest. The short-lived Heiji Rebellion was quickly crushed by Taira no Kiyomori, forcing Yoshitomo to flee the capital to Owari Province, where he was betrayed and killed by a retainer, apparently as he lay relaxing, unarmed at an *onsen* (spa).

**Above:** The priest Mongaku goads Minamoto Yoritomo into rebelling by showing him the skull of his father. *British Museum/Jo St Mart*

**Over page:** All scroll painting details from the Burning of the Sanjo Palace. **Top left:** Samurai protecting a royal carriage. **Below left:** Royalty being moved swiftly in his carriage. **Main picture:** Protecting a royal carriage. All *Burstein Collection/Corbis*

# Minamoto Yoshitsune
## (1159–1189)
### Heian/early Kamakura period military commander

Minamoto no Yoshitsune was a military commander in the late Heian and early Kamakura period, the ninth son of Minamoto no Yoshitomo. He is also one of the main characters in the Heike Monogatari (Tale of Heike), and perhaps "the epitome of a Japanese tragic hero."

Yoshitsune never knew his father, as he was born only shortly before the Heiji Rebellion of 1159 in which his father and oldest two brothers were killed. Along with brothers Yoritomo and Noriyori, he was saved from certain execution by the timely intervention of Taira no Kiyomori's stepmother, Lady Ikenozenni. Instead, Yoshitsune was brought up by the monks of Kurama Temple at Mount Hiei, near Kyoto. Later, he was sent to Hiraizumi in the far northern province of Mutsu, where his guardian was Fujiwara no Hidehira.

In 1180, Yoshitsune traveled south to join his brothers in the fight against the Taira. This was the first time they had met. With Noriyori, Yoshitsune commanded the Minamoto forces for most of the important battles in the Genpei Wars. In 1184 he marched south to recapture Kyoto from his cousin Minamoto no Yoshinaka, whom he subsequently defeated and killed at the battle of Awazu in Omi Province. The next month Yoshitsune and Noriyori defeated the Taira at

**Right:** Yoshitsune defeats Benki on Goto Bridge in Kyoto. Benki would become a devoted follower. *via Clive Sinclaire*

**Below and Below right:** Minamoto Yoshitsune is a popular figure in Japanese myth and legend. Here he is seen fleeing from his enemies with his older brother, Yoritomo. *via Clive Sinclaire*

**Right:** Minamoto Yoshitsune joined Yoritomo in the Genpei War of 1180. *British Museum/Jo St Mart*

**Below:** Triptych showing the "Ghosts of the Slain Taira Clan above the Ship of Yoshitsune" by Kuniyoshi, 1794. *Christie's Images/Corbis*

能光守教経
一條治郎忠頼

春亭画

Ichi-no-Tani, (to the west of modern Kobe, Hyogo). This victory was widely lauded, and henceforth Yoritomo sought to deprive his brother of further opportunities for glory. However, in March 1185, after a lull of several months in the fighting, Yoshitsune struck out again, leading an expedition across the Inland Sea to Shikoku, where he defeated the Taira again at their Yashima fortress. Then in April, he won a naval victory at the battle of Dan-no-ura (in present day Yamaguchi Prefecture), the final action of the Genpei Wars.

In the years following the Genpei Wars the rift between Yoritomo and Yoshitsune that had opened in the war widened to a gulf, and by 1189 the schism had erupted into open war. Motivated by jealousy for his sibling's successes against the Taira, and doubts as to his loyalty, Yoritomo declared him an enemy and forced him to flee, seeking the protection of Fujiwara no Hidehira in Mutsu. Yoshitsune was eventually surrounded by Yoritomo's troops at the fortress at Koromogawa no Tate. On June 13 he was forced to commit *seppuku* along with his wife and daughter. "Hot-tempered and subject to bad judgement in his personal life . . . he was a superb field commander and theater level strategist."

**Left:** Samurai warriors Ichijo Jiro Tadanori and Notonokami Noritsune locked in combat. The latter was known for a famous battle with Yoshitsune. *Library of Congress Prints and Photographs Division LC-DIG-jpd-00292*

# Minamoto no Yukiie
## (d. 1186)
### Heian Period military leader

Minamoto no Yukiie was one of the principal commanders of Minamoto no Yoshitomo's forces during the Genpei Wars. He was the brother of Minamoto Yoshitomo.

At the outbreak of the war, Yukiie was part of the initial plot to overthrow Taira Kiyomori and made efforts to rally forces in Kai and Shinano provinces. However, he initially displayed "the apathy of the Genji towards Yoritomo's cause" when the latter declared war against the Taira. Later he was persuaded to commit fully to the cause.

In 1181, Yukiie tried unsuccessfully to launch a surprise attack on Taira no Tomomori's camp at the Sunomatagawa, in Owari, but met with defeat. He retreated further into Owari and tried to take a stand at Yahagi-gawa, but his forces were defeated once more. Later in the war, Yukiie conspired with Minamoto no Yoshinaka against Yoritomo. Under this plot Minamoto no Yoshinaka planned to kidnap the cloistered Emperor Go-Shirakawa. In the event, Yukiie revealed the plot to Emperor Go-Shirakawa, who revealed it to Yoritomo. Consequently, Yukiie was decapitated in 1186 for treason.

**Below:** Minamoto Yukiie (on horseback) was defeated by Taira no Tomomori at the battle of Sunomatagawa, 1181. He escaped but was eventually betrayed and subsequently beheaded in 1186 on charges of high treason. *British Museum/Jo St Mart*

## Miura Yoshiatsu
**(d.1516)**
**Sengoku era military commander**

Miura Yoshiatsu was a late Sengoku era military commander, and a prominent member of the Miura clan of eastern Sagami Province, that had first risen to prominence in the Genpei Wars. In the ensuing years their influence waned.

Yoshiatsu was actually the son of Uesugi Takamasa, but was adopted by Miura Tokitaka as his heir before the birth of his own son. Yoshiatsu was then sent to live in a monastery, where he plotted to overthrow his erstwhile father.

In 1496 he attacked and killed Tokitaka and his son, and took up residence at Okazaki castle (in modern day Aichi Prefecture). He fought to contain the expansion of the Hojo clan under Hojo Soun, after the latter took Odawara castle. He was besieged at Okazaki in 1512 and fled to Arai castle, which fell to Hojo Soun in July 1516.

Yoshiatsu committed suicide along with Yoshimoto, the latter apparently cutting off his own head.

**Left:** Miura Yoshiatsu took refuge in the city of Arai, but his allies had deserted him and after a long siege the city fell in 1516. Yoshiatsu had little option but to commit *seppuku. British Museum/Jo St Mart*

## Mori Motonari
**(1497–1571)**
**Sengoku period Mori clan *daimyo***

Mori Motonari was an important daimyo in the west Chugoku region during the Sengoku period of the sixteenth century. He engineered the rise to power of the Mori clan. As a military commander he was wont to use guile and trickery, and through his schemes won many battles.

Motonari was born at Suzuo castle in Aki Province in western Honshu in 1497. He was the brother of Mori Okimoto, the *daimyo*, and after the latter's death in 1516 Motonari acted as guardian to Okimoto's heir, Mori Komatsumaru.

The Mori clan was a secondary power in Aki, subordinate to the Ouchi, Takeda, and Amago. Motonari's complex relations with these three powerful families, cordial and otherwise, would occupy most of his life.

His father, Hiromoto, had sworn nominal allegiance to the Ouchi in 1499, but under Okimoto these ties were broken. Beginning in 1516, Takeda Motoshige made attempts to exand into the Mori fief by assaulting their Koriyama citadel with a powerful host, but was trounced by the numerically inferior Mori forces under Motonari.

In 1522, war broke out between the Amago and Ouchi. Aki, which lay sandwiched between the rivals, was invaded by Amago Tsunehisa, and Motonari forced to submit. He was then ordered to attack the Takeda's Kagamiyama castle, in support of Tsunehisa's move against Kanayama. Ultimately, however, Motonari's efforts were in vain as Tsunehisa failed to bring down Kanayama and retreated.

In 1523, Komatsumaru himself died. In the aftermath of his death a dispute arose over who was to succeed. In the event, Motonari prevailed, and he thereafter strove to reunite the divided clan. Under Motonari's leadership, the clan drifted back into the Ouchi's camp, and he set about consolidating his own powerbase in Aki, and making allies among the other Aki chieftains.

The Amako subsequently made efforts to win back Motonari's support, but these were unsuccessful. Finally, in 1540, Amako Haruhisa invaded Aki with a large force, seeking to bring all of the province under

his control. Acknowledging that he stood little chance in the open field, Motonari fortified himself in Koriyama castle and held out for four months against the besieging army until relieved by Ouchi general Sue Harukata in early 1541.

In 1542, Ouchi Yoshitaka and Motonari launched a failed invasion of Izumo, seeking to take advantage of an Amako enemy weakened by recent defeat and the death of clan elder Tsunehisa. Although initially successful, the campaign bogged down and both commanders were forced to pull back.

He expanded the Mori presence in Bingo province, taking Takiyama in 1552 and strengthened his ties with the Murakami.

In 1554 Motonari annulled his long-standing but fragile alliance with Sue Harukata, who quickly despatched a powerful Sue army of 30,000 men to bring the Mori back into line. Motonari, with barely half that, nonetheless, defeated Sue troops at Oshikihata in June. In the summer of 1555, he scored a masterful victory at Miyajima against Harukata and with this became the most powerful lord in western Japan.

The following five years was marked by a series of battles with the powerful Otomo clan of Kyushu that began over Moji castle, a strategically important stronghold in the far northern tip of Buzen province. There was also much conflict with the Amago, who continued to resist all attempts to

**Above left:** In time Mori Motonari defeated his enemies and controlled the whole of Chugoku. *via Clive Sinclaire*

**Above:** As well as being a successful warrior and strategist Motonari (above left) was an influential patron of the arts and a significant poet. *British Museum/Jo St Mart*

subjugate them. In 1562 Motonari began a campaign of conquest against the Amago lord Yoshihisa. The Amago stronghold at Iwami was taken, and a campaign directed to cut another at Gassan-Toda off from its supply lines initiated. In the autumn of 1563 Mori invested Shiraga castle, and the castle surrendered in October after 70 days.

Gassan-Toda was now isolated, and in the spring of 1564 Motonari led a 25,000 army to lay siege. This first effort met with failure, but Motonari returned and finally, in January 1566, the castle surrendered. In a show of compassion Mori spared Yoshihisa's life, on the condition that he retire to a monastery.

Motonari died in 1571 at the age of 74, having established his name as one of the greatest warlords of the Sengoku *jidai*. The relatively insignificant clan which he had led for the greater part of the Sengoku *jidai* could by this time claim dominion over most of western Honshu.

## Mori Terumoto
### (1553–1625)
### Sengoku/early Edo period *daimyo*

Mori Terumoto was a *daimyo* in the western provinces during the late Sengoku and early Edo periods, and a military ally of Toyotomi Hideyoshi.

He was the grandson of Mori Motonari, and became *daimyo* of the clan upon his death. In line with his grandfather's wishes he made limited efforts to expand the already substantial Mori domain in the Chugoku region, but was soon drawn into conflict with Oda Nobunaga by offering support to the defenders of the Ishiyama Honganji. Terumoto sent his powerful navy to break the blockade, and though it succeeded in this, in 1578 his navy was defeated by a resurgent Nobunaga at the Second

116

battle of Kizawaguchi. Oda forces then occupied his domain. In 1582 Toyotomi Hideyoshi besieged his castle at Takamatsu, and Terumoto surrendered. After agreeing a peace treaty with Hideyoshi, he went on to participate in the Hideyoshi's Kyushu campaign and established Hiroshima castle.

In 1592, Hideyoshi appointed him to the *go-tairo* (council of five elders). In the dispute that prefaced the battle of Sekigahara, he sided against Tokugawa Ieyasu but was not present at the battle. He surrendered to Ieyasu at Osaka castle soon after, and had his domain drastically reduced to Nagato

**Above:** Fighting around Osaka castle after which Mori Terumoto was forced to surrender. A member of Hideyoshi's Council of Five Elders, Terumoto could mobilize more than 120,000 men into battle. *via Clive Sinclaire*

**Left:** Mori Terumoto was a good administrator but a poor general. *British Museum/Jo St Mart*

Province and Suÿ Province.

Terumoto is often portrayed as rather weak-willed, and a poor commander who generally subordinated military decisions to his retainers and other members of clan.

## Mori Yoshinari
### (1523–1570)
### Late Sengoku period military commander

Mori Yoshinari was an important retainer and military commander in the service of Oda Nobunaga during the late Sengoku period. He was born into the Mori clan of Owari Province, the eldest son of Mori Yoshiyuki. His early life is something of a mystery, but it seems that he served the Saito clan leader Dosan in Mino Province until the year of 1555, when he became one of Oba Nobunaga's

retainers. He fought at the siege of Kiyosu castle (in modern Aichi), and at Iwakura in 1558 and Okehazama in 1560. He then supported Nobunaga in his campaign against his former masters, the Saito, and for his services received Kanayama castle in 1565. He was with Nobunaga during the advance on Kyoto in 1568, and moved to Usayama castle in Omi Province.

In September 1570, an allied Asai and Asai army of 30,000 men attacked Otsu Province. Usayama castle was besieged and during the consequent battle of Anegawa, Yoshinari and his

eldest son, were killed. Yoshinari had three sons, one of who, Ranmaru, achieved fame as the loyal head page of Nobunaga, and died with him at Honnoji Temple in June 1582.

**Above:** Murakami Yoshikiyo (at right) fighting Takeda Shingen, aka "The Tiger of Kai." *British Museum/Jo St Mart*

**Left:** Mori Yoshinari (standing) He was killed fighting the Asai and Asakura near Otsu in 1570. *British Museum/Jo St Mart*

## Murakami Yoshikiyo
(1501–1573)
### Sengoku era Murakami *daimyo*

Murakami Yoshikiyo was a Sengoku era *daimyo* of the Murakami clan of northern Shinano (modern Nagano Prefecture), and a trusted ally of Uesugi Kenshin against the Takeda. The Shinano Murakami, who claimed descent from Minamoto Yorinobu, had risen by the beginning of the Sengoku *jidai* to become one of the most powerful families in

Shinano. Yoshikiyo was born at the Murakami's Katsurao castle and succeeded his father as head of the clan in the early 1520s.

In 1541 he formed an alliance with the Suwa and Takeda against the other Shinano clans. However, as Yoshikiyo sought to further his influence in Shinano, an inevitable conflict of interests arose between him and Takeda Shingen. With the Suwa, Ogasawara, and Kiso, he resolved to try to check Shingen's expansion. In March 1542 the tripartite alliance was soundly defeated by Shingen's forces at the battle of Sezawa (Shinano).

Then, in February 1548, the Takeda and Murakami met again at the battle of Uedahara in southern Shinano. Although Yoshikiyo won this encounter, his triumph was shortlived. In August, at the battle of Shiojiritoge, Shingen defeated Yoshikiyo's ally Ogasawara Nagatoki. In 1551 Toishi castle fell to the Takeda, and two years later they moved on Katsurao castle. Weakened by the loss of his castles, Yoshikiyo fled north to Echigo, where was given refuge by Uesugi Kenshin.

Under Kenshin, Yoshikiyo fought many more times against Shingen, most notably the series of battles at Kawanakajima. For his loyal service he was given a domain in Echigo Province and died at Nechi castle there in 1573.

**Above:** Naito Masatoyo died honorably in battle after being shot many times with arrows and then beheaded. *via Jo StMart*

**Right:** Nitta Yoshisada is said to have died in the siege of Kuromaru when his horse fell dead, trapping him underneath. Unable to escape, Nitta drew his short sword and cut off his own head. *British Museum/Jo St Mart*

# Naito Masatoyo
**(1522–1575)**
**Sengoku era military commander**

Naito Masatoyo was a Sengoku era military commander under Takeda Shingen, one of the famous 24 generals and veteran of many of the Takeda clan's battles. Masatoyo was son of Kudo Toratoyo, senior retainer of Takeda Nobutora, and was known initially as Kudo Sukenaga. His father fell from grace with Nobutora, and was killed by him as a direct result. After Nobutora himself was deposed the Kudo were reinstated and formally excused. Subsequently, Sukenaga too on a senior rank in Takeda's army. In 1566 he was given Minowa castle in Kozuke Province and later fought at Mikatagahara and at Nagashino (1575). In the course of the latter action he was was killed.

# Nitta Yoshisada
**(1301–1338)**
**Head of the Nitta clan**

Nitta Yoshisada was the head of the Nitta clan of Kozuke in the late Kamakura and early Muromachi periods. He was an important supporter of Emperor Go-Daigo's Southern Court in the *Nanboku-cho* period (the Northern and Southern Courts period), which lasted from 1336 to 1392.

The Nitta clan could claim descent from the *Seiwa Genji* (the most successful branch of the Minamoto clan) and were well-established opponents of the Kamakura shogunate, and the regents of the Hojo clan. In part, this was because the ancestor of the clan, Minamoto no Yoshishige, had failed to give his backing to Minamoto Yoritomo in the Genpei War a century earlier, and the Nitta were never admitted to the Kamakura clique.

In 1331, the Emperor Go-Daigo and his son Prince Morinaga began scheming to bring down the shogunate, a necessary step in his ambitious plans to re-establish the power of the Imperial throne. His plans were discovered, precipitating the Genko Incident, which quickly developed into open war. The *bakufu* sent a force from Kamakura to censure him, and in April 1332 the Emperor was exiled to Oki Province (the Oki Islands in modern-day Shimane Prefecture). The following year he escaped and with Morinaga began raising an army against the shogunate. In 1333, Go-Daigo recaptured Kyoto, while Nitta Yoshisada led forces from across Japan against the regent, Hojo Takatoki, at the Kamakura citadel on Inamura Cape. The capital fell on July 5 after a three-week siege, bringing to an end the Kamakura Shogunate. The *Taiheiki* (a fourteenth century Japanese epic) says that before the final assault, Nitta

**Right:** In his final battle Nitta Yoshisada cuts the arrows from the air as his horse is shot dead under him. *via Clive Sinclaire*

期最の貞

## Niwa Nagahide
(1535–1585)
**Sengoku and early Azuchi-Momoyama period** *daimyo*

Niwa Nagahide was a *daimyo* and military commander during the later Sengoku and early Azuchi-Momoyama periods, and an important retainer to the Oda clan.

Nagahide was born in Owari Province, the second son of Niwa Nagamasa. At the age of fifteen he began his lifelong service with Oda Nobunaga, and in time he rose to become one of Nobunaga's senior retainers, seemingly one of the few he genuinely trusted. He fought in many of Nobunaga's campaigns, notably the siege of Sawayama (Omi) in 1571 and against Asai Nagamasa at Odani castle. He also fought at the battle of Nagashino in 1575, afterwards directing the construction of Azuchi castle, on the shores of Lake Biwa, from where Nobunaga could guard the approaches to Kyoto. For his services Nagahide was given Wakasa Province and Sawayama castle in Omi.

In 1582, Nobunaga ordered Nagahide to embark on a campaign against Chosogabe Motochika in Shikoku, but rapidly withdrew on receiving news of Nobunaga's assassination by Akechi Mitsuhide at the Honnoji. He helped Toyotomi Hideyoshi avenge his master's death at the battle of Yamasaki in July. Nagahide thereafter lent his support to Hideyoshi; in 1583 he helped in the conclusive defeat of Shibata Katsuie at Shizugatake, for which he was

threw his "gold-mounted sword" into the sea and prayed to the sun goddess of Ise (Amaterasu, the mythical founder of Japan), who drew back the waters before Inamura Cape, facilitating Yoshisada's entrance to the city

For his service in bringing down the shogunate, Yoshisada received Hojo lands in Echigo, Harima, and Kozuke provinces. However, all was not well, for during the early years of the Kemmu Restoration rivalry between Prince Morinaga, Yoshisada, and the wily and ambitious Ashikaga Takauji turned to open conflict. In August 1335 Takauji had Morinaga assassinated and in the following month installed himself as *shogun* at

Kamakura. Very soon he was inciting against Yoshisada, prompting Go-Daigo to denounce him as an enemy of the throne. In June 1336 Yoshisada lost the battle at Minatogawa, presaging the division of the country under the Namboku-cho jidai. Yoshisada's last battle came at Kuromaru castle, at Fujishima in Echizen, in August 1338. Leading a small against *kanrei* (deputy) Shiba Takatsune he received a mortal arrow wound.

**Above:** Yoshisada offers his sword to Amaterasu. *Jo StMart*

**Right:** Niwa Nagahide (front center) supporting Oda Nobunaga at the battle of Nagashino. *British Museum/Jo St Mart*

given Echizen and Kaga, and sent a Niwa army under his son Nagashige to fight in the Komaki campaign against Sasa Narimasa. In 1585, Nagahide died at the age of forty, by then one of the most powerful *daimyo* in Japan. Although it is generally told that he died of natural causes, there has been speculation that Nagahide committed suicide, brought on by feelings of guilt that he had somehow failed his revered master.

## Obata Toramori
### (1491–1561)
### Sengoku period commander

Obata Toramori was a military commander of the Takeda clan during the later Sengoku period. He initially served Takeda Nobutora and after Nobutora's death, his son, Shingen. Toramori was one of the Takeda's

"Twenty-Four Generals," but usually fought as a subordinate of more senior retainers (notably Baba Nobufusa). During his military career, he reputedly fought in thirty battles, and was wounded countless times. His last action was at the final battle at Kawanakajima in 1561, the climax of a protracted series of engagements against Uesugi Kenshin. After the battle, his health already in decline, he retired to his Kaizu castle and died.

**Below:** Obata Toramori fighting for Takeda Shingen. *Jo StMart*

# Oda Nobuhide
### (1510–1551)
### Leader of the Oda clan

Oda Nobuhide was leader of the Oda clan of Owari during the Sengoku era, and made strident but ultimately unsuccessful attempts to unite the divided clan. He is best remembered however as the father of Oda Nobunaga. Nobuhide was born at Shobata castle in the Kaito district of Owari, the eldest son of Oda Nobusada. As the head of the Oda clan, sought to expand into neighboring Mino and Mikawa. In prosecuting these aspirations, he had numerous clashes with Saito Dosan, *daimyo* of Mino province, the Matsudaira of Mikawa and Imagawa Yoshimoto, *daimyo* of Suruga and Totomi.

In November 1540, he captured Anjo castle in Mikawa Province, and in September 1542 defeated the Imagawa in an engagement at Azukizaka. Also in 1542, he launched a campaign against Saito Dosan in Mino. Although he enjoyed some successes in Mino, a loss at Kanoguchi in 1547 presaged a decline in his fortunes, culminating in 1548 with a heavy defeat at the hands of a joint Imagawa/Matsudaira force at the second battle of Azukizaka.

Nobuhide subsequently made his peace with Saito Dosan by marrying his son, Nobunaga, to Saito's daughter, Nohime. Supported by Dosan, Nobuhide continued to battle with the Imagawa until his death in 1551.

# Oda Nobunaga
## (1534–1582)
### Sengoku era *daimyo* and military commander

Oda Nobunaga was a late Sengoku era *daimyo* and military commander, one of the three so-called unifiers of Japan and thus a crucial figure in the country's history. He began the process of "fusion," to use Stephen Turnbull's term, that ultimately led to the end of the Sengoku *jidai* and founding of the Tokugawa shogunate.

Nobunaga was born at Nagoya castle, the second son of Oda Nobuhide, a deputy *shugo* (military governor) in Owari Province. In his teenage years he established a reputation for eccentric behavior, earning him the nickname *Owari no Otsuke* (the "Fool of Owari"). His reputation among the Oda retainers was made all the worse by an ill-judged act at his father's funeral in 1551 at Bansyoji (in present day Kori Town, Fukushima prefecture), when he is said to have thrown the ceremonial incense at the altar. Thereafter many within the Oda assemblage began to favor the other brother, Nobuyuki, to succeed, although Nobunaga (as the eldest son) was the legitimate heir.

To consolidate his own power within the clan, Nobunaga arrived at the simple expedient of eliminating the opposition, beginning with Oda Nobutomo at Kiyosu castle. In 1556, Nobuyuki, with the support of Shibata Katsuie and Hayashi Hidesada, made an attempt to wrest control of the clan from his brother. The conspirators were defeated at the battle of Ino, and spared. The next year, however, Nobuyuki began to machinate again. His plot was exposed and this time Nobunaga showed less mercy, ordering Nobuyuki to be slain at Kiyosu. Several other suspected opponents were dispatched in the following years and by the end of the decade, having secured his authority over the clan and Owari province, Nobunaga was able to focus on the program of expansion begun by his father.

Already, in 1558, he had clashed with the rival Imagawa clan at Terabe, a fight that he lost. Then, in 1560, he had to face off an invasion of Owari by a powerful Imagawa army led by Yoshimoto. His masterful victory against Yoshimoto at Okezahama, against all odds, marked the beginning of his irresistible rise in power and influence. In 1561, Nobunaga made his peace with Matsudaira Motoyasu (later Tokugawa Ieyasu), ending the long friction between the two clans. That same year he began a campaign against the Saito clan in Mino, that was mourning the loss of clan leader Yoshitatsu. In June, Nobunaga defeated them at Moribe and established himself at Komaki castle, using this as a base from which to coordinate further advances into Mino. He progressively undermined the Saito through intrigues with their retinue, and finally defeated them in 1567 at the siege of Inabayama castle.

The following year Nobunaga received Ashikaga Yoshiaki at Gifu castle, come to solicit his support for a campaign against the usurpers of his brother, *shogun* Ashikaga Yoshiteru.

Seizing the opportunity to enter Kyoto with an official mandate, and gain a means to justify future conquests, Nobunaga launched a campaign. He quashed the opposition of the Rokkaku in southern Omi Province and was soon at the city limits. The usurpers were forced to flee, and Yoshiaki installed as the new *shogun*—albeit as a puppet with strictly limited powers. Soon, however, Yoshiaiki grew resentful of Nobunaga's rigid control, and set about forging alliances with opponents of Nobunaga's regime.

The two most notable of them were the Asakura and the Azai, both with deep-seated resentments toward the upstart Oda clan. Uncowed, in 1570 Nobunaga took Odani and Yokoyama castles and shortly after defeated a combined Asakura/Azai army at the battle of Anegawa.

Nobunaga now vented his spleen on the Enryaku-ji monastery on Mt. Hiei, home to the recalcitrant Tendai faction of *sohei* (warrior monks), which formed another of locus of opposition. In 1571 Nobunaga mercilessly attacked and burned the monastery, killing between 3,000 and 4,000 men, women, and children. In May of the same year he began his epic siege of the *Ikko-ikki* stronghold at Nagashima, which was to frustrate him repeatedly over the next three years.

In 1572, Nobunaga faced a challenge from his nominal ally, Takeda Shingen, who took up the *shogun*'s mandate for a move on the capital. He began his campaign with an invasion of Tokugawa Ieysau's domain, and

won a battle at Mikatagahara in 1573. Not long after, Shingen suddenly died, and the theat faded away—somewhat fortuitously in fact, for this allowed Nobunaga to bring bring pressure to bear on Yoshiaki. The *shogun*'s weak forces were shortly defeated and Yoshiaki himself sent into exile, thus ending the reign of the Ashikaga shogunate.

With the final destruction of the Asai and Nagamasa in 1573, and the Nagashima in 1574, the only viable opposition to Nobunaga remaining was the Takeda clan, under the steerage of Katsuyori since Shingen's untimely death.

In June 1575, two mighty armies, on one side the combined forces of Nobunaga and Tokugawa Ieyasu and on the other the Takeda, clashed at the epic battle of Nagashino. The combined forces of Nobunaga and Tokugawa Ieyasu devastated the outmoded Takeda army with the skilled use of *arquebusiers*.

Often hailed as a turning point in Japanese history, Nobunaga used his victory at Nagashino as a springboard for continued expansion. He sent Shibata Katsuie and Maeda Toshiie to the north and Akechi Mitsuhide to attack Tamba Province, while he himself continued in his efforts to bring down Ishiyama Hongan-ji. Frustrated by Mori Motonari's endeavors to

**Above**: Oda Nobunaga (holding the fan) remonstrates with general Akechi Mitsuhide. The latter was Oda's retainer and the pair quarrelled frequently, leading Mitsuhide eventually to betray Nobunaga and force him to commit *seppuku*. *British Museum/Jo St Mart*

provision the complex by sea, in 1577, Nobunaga ordered Toyotomi Hideyoshi to begin a campaign against the Mori clan in Chugoku.

That same year Nobunaga met with a rare reversal at the hands of Uesugi Kenshin, in the battle of Tedorigawa. Buoyed by his success, Kenshin began preparations for an advance on the capital, causing Nobunaga to realign his forces and

call a temporary halt to his program of expansion in Noto, Kaga, and Etchu provinces. However, the sudden and untimely death of Kenshin, and the confusion that gripped the Uesugi thereafter, let Nobunaga kick-start his campaign in this area again.

In 1580, the stoic defenders of the Ishiyama Hongan-ji were finally persuaded to surrender and within two years he had overwhelmed another locus of opposition, the Takeda clan.

By now he was at the pinnacle of his career, by some measure the most powerful warlord in Japan and poised to embark on invasions of Shikoku and the Uesugi domain in Echigo. But at this crowning point in his illustrious career, things took a strange and unforeseen turn, which had a profound effect on the subsequent history of Japan. In 1582, as part of the ongoing effort against the Mori clan in Chugoku, Toyotomi Hideyoshi invaded Bitchu, and attempted to bring down their Takamatsu castle. Determined to hold on to this strategically important bastion, Mori Terumoto sent in reinforcements, and a stalemate ensued. Messengers were duly dispatched from Hideyoshi's camp calling to Nobunaga for reinforcements of his own. Breaking off from a victorious tour in the Kansai with Tokugawa Ieyasu, Nobunaga made preparations to lead an army to Takamatsu. On the night of June 20/21, while en route for the Chugoku region, Nobunaga stayed at a favored resting place, the Honno-ji temple in Kyoto, accompanied by a small band of servants and bodyguards.

At dawn the next morning Nobunaga woke to find the temple surrounded by a large force under

his erstwhile retainer, Akechi Mitsuhide. The events that followed are somewhat muddied, but it seems that Nobunaga resolved, or was forced, to commit *seppuku*. Together with him died his teenage page (*o-kosho*), Mori Ranmaru (son of Motonari), who had served him faithfully for many years. Meanwhile, Akechi forces assaulted Nijo castle, and Mitsuhide declared himself the new *shogun*. However, eleven days after the coup, Toyotomi Hideyoshi's army caught Mitsuhide at Yamazaki, where he was defeated and killed.

Toyotomi eventually emerged as Nobunaga's successor.

Nobunaga's life impacted on a great many areas of Japanese society, and his legacy can be seen in many of its instituitions and customs. Militarily, he revolutionized warfare in Japan, through introduction of new weapons and tactics. In the political sphere he championed a system of meritocratic administration, wherein appointments were based on ability, over the nepotism that had previously held sway. Under this administration, foundations were laid that formed the basis for the Tokugawa shogunate; and in the area of economics, Nobunaga encouraged the development of international trade, beyond China and the Korean peninsula, to Europe, the Philippines, Siam, and Indonesia.

Although often depicted as a brutal man, culturally, he bequeathed a fine body of works. He built extensive gardens and castles, including the magnificent Azuchi castle, and popularized *ocha* (the tea ceremony). Under Nobunaga we can see the beginnings of modern kabuki theater and he introduced aspects of European art and culture. His grave is at Mount Koya, in modern Wakayama Prefecture.

## Ogasawara Nagatoki
### (1519–1583)
### *Daimyo* in Shinano Province

Ogasawara Nagatoki was a *daimyo* in Shinano Province during the later Sengoku era, and an ally of Uesugi Kenshin in his epic battles against the Takeda clan.

His clan traced their lineage to Takeda Yoshikiyo, who had served Minamoto Yoritomo in the Genpei Wars, and was gifted lands in Shinano by Ashikaga Takauji. The center of their domain was Fukashi castle. In 1541, Nagatoki joined with the Suwa for a punitive strike into Kai against the Takeda, but they were defeated at Nirasaki (in modern Yamanashi Prefecture).

The next year, Nagatoki formed an alliance with the other Shinano *daimyo* (Murakami Yoshikiyo, Suwa Yorishige, and Kiso Yoshiyasu) to try to resist Takeda Shingen's advance into Shinano Province. The rival camps faced up at Sezawa on March 9, 1542, but Nagatoki and his allies were conclusively beaten and unable to prevent Shingen overrunning the province.

Nagatoki, now landless, allied himself with the only *daimyo* in the Kanto *chiho* (area or region) with the power to resist Takeda, Uesugi Kenshin. In 1545 he fought alongside Takato Yoritsugu in his failed defense of Takato castle. (in modern Nagano Prefecture), and three years later lost another encounter with Shingen at the battle of Shiojiritoge. The final defeat of a rather checkered military

career came the following year with the loss of Fukashi. Nagatoki ended his life in Kyoto, as a tutor to prospective samurai.

**Left:** In 1551 Sorin met Francis Xavier and allowed the establishment of a Jesuit mission on his lands. While his motivation for supporting Christianity is unknown, he and his wife embraced the religion and he is known to us as the Christian *daimyo*. *Jo stmart*

## Otomo Sorin
**(1530–1587)**
**Sengoku period *daimyo***

Otomo Sorin was *daimyo* of the Otomo clan during the later Sengoku *jidai*, who worked to unify much of Kyushu under his control. He was a also a key player The Otomo had been one of the major clans in Kyushi since the Yamato *jidai*, and held important military posts within the court since that time.

Sorin, who was born under the name Yoshishige, was descended directly from Fujiwara Hidesato, a Heian era military commander who served Minamoto no Yoritomo during the Genpei Wars. His father was Otomo Yoshiaki, lord of Funai.

During the late fifteenth and early sixteenth centuries feuding between the Otomo and other local clans, notably the Shoni, Tawara, and Tachibana, colored events in Kyushu. In 1550 Yoshiaki was murdered by one of his own retainers and, as his eldest son, Sorin succeeded as head of the clan. Sorin moved quickly to expand the Otomo domain; in 1551 he fought and defeated Kikuchi Yoshimune of Higo. Six years later, however, came the first of a series of battles that he fought with the Mori clan over possession of Moji castle in Buzen. The castle fell to the Mori in 1558, only for Sorin to retake it the following September. Moji exchanged hands once again soon after, and all subsequent attempts by Yoshishige to reclaim this strategic prize failed, and Moji remained in Mori hands.

In 1562 Sorin forged an alliance with the Amako for an attack on the Mori holdings in Buzen. Over the course of the next decade he put down the rebellious Akizuki of Chikuzen, and fought a disastrous engagement against the Ryuzoji of Hizen at Imayama, prompting another war with the Mori clan. By the end of the decade he had the Mori on the defensive, and could claim control of much of northern Kyushu.

The early 1570s were a time of comparative peace and retrenchment, during which Sorin continued to use his influence to encourage the spread of Christianity throughout his domain. In 1576 Sorin passed formal control of the clan over to his son,

Yoshimune, and assumed the name Francisco.

Two years later, a crisis erupted in Hyuga Province, where the Shimazu clan under Yoshihisa had overwhelmed the incumbent *daimyo*, Ito Yoshisuke, and forced him to seek asylum in the Otomo domain. Determined to face off this threat, Yoshimune and Tawara Chikataka, gathered up their armies and marched into Hyuga, with Sorin following on with his own troops.

Yoshihisa rallied an army and brought it north. On December 10, 1578, the two armies met at Mimigawa (in modern Miyazaki). The battle was a catastrophe for the Otomo: thousands of their troops were killed and the others scattered, and the Otomo army fell back in disorder to Bungo. After this, the fortunes of the Otomo went into a rapid and seemingly terminal decline. The following year the Ryuzoji took advantage of their badly weakened state to drive the Otomo out of Chikugo, and elsewhere the Akizuki clan rose in rebellion. Bungo itself was soon in a fractious state, and the Otomo forced to agree terms with Shimazu Yoshihisa.

In May 1586, now in the autumn of his years, Sorin traveled to Osaka seeking an audience with Toyotomi Hideyoshi, from whom he was able to secure assistance against Shimazu. This was proved to be a judicious decision; in November, the Shimazu invaded Otomo lands in Bungo again. In December 1586 the first elements of a massive Toyotomi host landed on Kyushu and pushed the Shimazu all

the way back to Satsuma. Sorin died later that year, content in the knowledge that his clan was restored to its lands.

## Otomo Yoshimune
### (1558–1605)
*Daimyo* and last head of the Otomo clan

Otomo Yoshimune was a late Sengoku and early Edo era daimyo, the last head of the Otomo clan, and one of Toyotomi Hideyoshi's principal commanders during the campaigns in Korea. However, his name is forever associated with a purported act of cowardice during the campaign that saw him exiled and stripped off his lands.

In 1576, Otomo Sorin relinquished control of the clan to his eighteen-year old son, Yoshimune. During his rather checkered tenure, Yoshimiune led the disastrous campaign in Hyuga Province against the Shimazu, and was heavily defeated by them at Mimigawa. In subsequent years Yoshimune faced many challenges to his authority from rebellious vassals.

Through the diplomatic efforts of his father, Sorin, Yoshimune obtained the promise of military assisatance from Toyotomi Hideyoshi against the Shimazu. In November 1586, the Shimazu invaded Bungo, and an expeditionary force was quickly sent to his aid. However, during the subsequent campaigning, Yoshimune bungled an attempt to relieve Toshimitsu castle, and was soundly beaten at Hetsugigawa in January 1587. Yoshimune was forced out of Funai, and only saved by the timely arrival of Hideyoshi's main army, which drove the Shimazu back to southern Kyushu.

During the first campaign in Korea in 1592, Yoshimune fought with Kuroda Nagamasa's division, but disgraced himself in the actions around Pyong'yang. Tasked with the defense of an important fort Yoshimune seems to have lost his nerve for the fight in the face of a determined Chinese force. He failed to respond to a plea from Konishi Yukinaga for aid and abandoned the position to the enemy. For this he was condemned for cowardice and lost all of his lands in Kyushu.

At Sekigahara, Yoshimune fought with Ishida Mitsunari, and after was sent into exile. He died in September 1605.

**Right:** Otomo Yoshimune fighting in the battle of Mimigawa, 1578. He survived, but was on the losing side which encouraged his vassals to rebel. He was the last lord of Otomo. *British Museum/Jo St Mart*

# Ouchi Yoshioki
**(1477–1528)**
**Early Sengoku era *daimyo***

Ouchi Yoshioki was an early Sengoku era *daimyo* in Suo, Nagato, and Iwami, and *kanrei* to *shogun* Ashika Yoshitane. Since the fourteenth century, the Ouchi clan had grown to become a major power in western Honshu, from where they controlled trade with the continent. During his tenure, Yoshioki maintained efforts to increase the power and influence of the clan, provoking clashes with other Kyushu clans, notably the Otomo of Bungo and the Amako of Izumo. In 1508 Yoshioki led an army to Kyoto, to restore the recently deposed shogun, Ashikaga Yoshitane, and was thereafter elevated to the position of *kanrei*. He settled in Kyoto and there resided for the next ten years.

In 1511 (with Hosokawa Takakuni) he defeated a resurgent challenge to the shogunate by Hosokawa Masataka and Hosokawa Sumimoto at Funaokayama, north of Kyoto. In 1518 Yoshioki was forced to return to Yamaguchi, to face off the ambitions of the Amako, beginning a rivalry between himself and Amako Tsunehisa that would endure until he died in 1528. They fought campaigns in Aki (1522) and Iwami provinces.

**Right:** Ouchi Yoshioki in the thick of battle.
*British Museum/Jo St Mart*

# Sakai Tadatsugu
## (1527–1596)
### Sengokua era military commander

Sakai Tadatsugu was a leading military commander in the service of Tokugawa Ieyasu during the Sengoku era. He was one of an elite group known as the "Four Guardians of the Tokugawa." Tadatsugu's clan were vassals of the Matsudaira in Mikawa, and in 1560, when Matsudaira Motoyasu severed his ties with the Imagawa—with the help of Tadatsugu, who was made the castellan of the Yoshida castle. He fought many subsequent battles with Motoyasu's son Tokugawa Ieyasu, notably at Mikatagahara in 1573. During the headlong retreat from the battlefield he cool-headedly pulled off a bluff that prevented his pursuers from taking Hamamatsu castle.

Tadatsugu was at Nagashino two years later and during the Komaki campaign in 1584, he successfully turned back a move by Mori Nagayoshi against Kiyosu castle. After the Odawara campaign was successfully concluded, he received a modest fief at Takasaki. Tadatsugu died in Kyoto in the winter of 1596.

**Right:** One of the "Four Guardians of the Tokugawa," Sakai Tadatsugu was a successful and favorite commander serving Tokugawa Ieyasu in the late-Sengoku period. *British Museum/Jo St Mart*

# Sanada Yukimura
(1567–1615)
Late Sengoku/early Edo era
military commander

Sanada Yukimura was a late Sengoku and early Edo era military commander, a one-time a retainer of the Takeda who later served under Toyotomi Hideyoshi. His peers held him in high regard as a warrior; Shimazu Tadatsune, for example, called him the best warrior in Japan and Hideyoshi himself was lavish with praise for the man.

He was the second son of Sanada Masayuki, a retainer of the Takeda clan. After the final defeat of the Takeda in 1582, the Sanada became independent, eventually allying with Toyotomi Hideyoshi. In the run-up to Sekigahara, the clan's allegiances were split. Masayuki and Yukimura stood for Ishida Mitsunari, while Yukimura's brother, Nobuyuki, sided with Tokugawa Ieyasu. In the subsequent fighting Masayuki and Yukimura defended Ueda castle against an army led by Tokugawa Hidetada, delaying him before Sekigahara.

In the aftermath Yukimura and his father narrowly missed being executed and were sent into exile to Kudoyama. Although his father died in captivity, Yukimura escaped to answer the rallying call of the Toyotomi at Osaka castle. During the winter siege of Osaka, Yukimura commanded *arquebusiers* through a spirited defense. Outnumbered, and weakened by a wound, he was eventually killed.

# Sanada Yukitaka
(1512–1574)
Sengoku era military commander

Sanada Yukitaka was a Sengoku era military commander under Takeda Shigen, a noted strategist, one of Shingen's band of twenty-four generals, and *daimyo* of Shinano.

Although it is known that Yukitaka was born in Shinano province, his father's identity is unclear. Some accounts suggest Uno Munetsuna, who was a Shinano *daimyo*.

Initially Yukitaka fought under the Uno in battles with the neighboring Murakami and Suwa clans, and in 1541 lost his Sanada castle to their united armies. After this reversal Yukitaka entered the service of the Nagano clan of Kozuke. Around 1544, he switched his allegiance again—this time to Takeda Shingen—and as a result, Yukitaka was able to reclaim Sanada castle in around 1550.

He was a noted strategist and assisted Shingen on numerous occasions, most notably at the battle of Odaihara in 1546, and the capture of Toishi in 1550. He went on to fight at the fourth battle of Kawanakajima (1561) and died of illness a year after Shingen.

**Overleaf:** Shimazu Tadatsune (the fearless *daimyo* of Satsuma), called Sanada Yukimura (left) the "Number one warrior in Japan." Others called him "A Hero who may appear once in hundred years" and "Crimson demon of war." *British Museum/Jo St Mart*

## Sasa Narimasa
### (1539–1588)
### Military commander during the Sengoku jidai

Narimasa was an important military commander under Oda Nobunaga during the Sengoku *jidai*, along with Maeda Toshiie and Fuwa Mitsuharu, he was one of the so-called *sanninshu*. He helped to evolve many of the tactics that Nobunaga used in his pioneering employment of *arquebusiers* on the battlefield, but later fell foul of Hideyoshi and was force to commit *seppuku*. Narimasa served Nobunaga from his early career in Owari Province, helping to defeat the Asai and Asakura at the battle of Anegawa in July 1570. He was at Mikatagahara three years later when Nobunaga was defeated by Takeda Shingen, and helped Nobunaga to avenge this defeat at Nagashino. In 1580 he was employed against the Uesugi in Etchu, and was officially gifted the province the following year for his service. In 1582 he moved to eradicate the last Uesugi outposts in Etchu, and was preparing for an invasion of Ehigo at the time of Nobunaga's death. He fought under Shibata Katsuie against Toyotomi Hideyoshi during the Shizugatake campaign, and the next year fought Hideyoshi

**Left:** Sasa Narimasa (front center) at the first battle of Azukizaka, 1542. In later battles he was given command of arquebus troops thanks to his skill in gunnery tactics. *British Museum/Jo St Mart*

again under Tokugawa Ieyasu in the Komaki campaign. During this latter campaign he was ordered to take Suemori castle in Noto from his friend Maeda Toshiie.

When faced with the irresistible advance of Hideyoshi on Etchu in 1585, Narimasa was compelled to surrender. He lost all his lands in Etchu but was compensated with a smaller fief in Higo, on the under-standing that he govern it according to strict guidelines. Narimasa chafed under the yoke, and set about foment-ing a rebellion among the Higo samu-rai. As a punishment for his disloyalty he was compelled to commit *seppuku*.

## Sasaki Takatsuna
**(1160–1214)**
### Commander in the Genpei War

Famous for his race against Kajiwara Kagesue to be first across the River Uji in 1184, a commander in the Genpei War, Sasaki Takatsuna sided with Minamoto no Yoritomo against the Tiara. He saved his lord's life at Ishibashiyama and was promoted to be governor of Nagato *rovince. However, he is said to have retired in 1195 to become a priest and died in 1214.

**Right:** Wearing his magnificent *o-yoroi* (great armor) Sasaki Takatsuna gallops on Shogun Yoritomo's white horse, Ikezuki, to be the first into battle across the Uji river during the Genpei Wars. *via Clive Sinclaire*

140

**Below:** At the battle of Ishibashiyama Sasaki Takatsuna saved Minamoto no Yoritomo's life and helped to destroy the Taira clan. His reward was the position of *shugo* (governor) of Nagato Province. *via Clive Sinclaire*

**Below:** Shibata Katsuiie served Toyotomi Hideyoshi (see page 145). *via Clive Sinclaire*

# Satomi Yoshitaka
## (1512–1574)
### Sengoku era *daimyo*

Satomi Yoshitaka was a Sengoku era *daimyo* with major land holdings on the Boso peninsula in Awa. Yoshitaka was the eldest son of Satomi Sanetaka, who had a long-running enmity with the Hojo clan. In 1533 Sanetaka was overthrown in a coup led by his nephew Yoshitoyo, and compelled to commit suicide. Yoshitaka succeeded him, and moved swiftly to avenge his father, consolidate his control over the clan, and expand its dominion. The following year, in 1534, Yoshitaka led a force to besiege his father's killer, Yoshitoyo, at Inamura castle. Emulating the punishment Yoshitoyo had dealt Sanetaka, Yoshitaka demanded that he kill himself.

The continuing friction with the Hoko prompted him to ally with *shogun* Ashikaga Yoshiaki for a planned attack on the Hojo fortifications in Musashi. In November 1538, while the Hojo were preoccupied with fighting the Imagawa, Yoshitoyo and Yoshiaki attacked the Hojo's outlying Musashi forts. Hojo Ujitsuna quickly rallied a force from Izu and Sagami and marched north to confront the threat. The two forces met at Konodai; the allied Satomi/Ashikaga forces was roundly defeated and Yoshitaka chased back onto the Boso Peninsula.

Yoshitaka, now on the defensive, held off an attempted Hojo incursion in 1540. He spent most of the ensuing decade retrenching, and thereafter made some limited gains, including Shiizu castle. In 1560 the Hojo attacked Awa again, and Yoshitaka had to appeal to Uesugi Kenshin for assistance. While Kenshin led an attack into the Kanto region, Yoshitaka sent his ships against the Hojo fleet off Miura (Sagami). Yoshitaka fought his last battle with the Hojo three years later, again at Konodai, where the heavily outnumbered Satomi forces tried and failed to lure Hojo Ujitsuna's advancing army into a trap. Satomi's young son was killed in the battle, although Yoshitaka himself lived on until 1574. His sons continued to resist the Hojo, but the clan died out in 1622.

**Above:** Satomi Yoshitaka at right. *British Museum/Jo St Mart*
**Right:** Shibata Katsuie fighting against Oda Nobunaga at the battle of Ino. Katsuie was on the losing side but was spared his life after swearing allegiance to Nobunaga as his overlord. *via Clive Sinclaire*

144

## Shibata Katsuiie
### (1522–1583)
### Sengoku era military commander

Shibata Katsuiie was a military commander during the Sengoku era, remembered as one of Oda Nobunaga's most accomplished generals.

Katsuie was born into the Owari brach of the Shibata family, descendants of one of Minamoto Yoritomo's retainers. They eventually came to serve the Oda clan and in the succession dispute that erupted after the death of Nobuhide between his sons Nobunaga and Nobuyuki, Katsuiie threw his support behind Oda Nobuyuki. Together, in 1556, they launched a failed coup d'état against Nobunaga, which culminated in defeat at the battle of Ino. Nobuyuki was killed, but Katsuiie was spared, on condition that he accepted Nobunaga as suzerain. After Nobunaga had united Owari, Katsuiie fought in his army against the Imagawa at Okehazama in June 1560 and in the campaigns against the Saito clan in Mino.

In 1567, Shibata invaded Settsu province and defeated an allied Miyoshi/Matrunaga army near Sakai. Three years after that he fought what is perhaps his most famous action, at the siege of Chokoji castle in southern Omi. In advance of his summer 1570 campaign against the Asai and Asakura clans, Nobunaga had installed Katsuiie and 400 troops at this strategically important stronghold. An overwhelmingly larger army under Rokkaku Yoshitaka soon besieged them. Katsuiie's men resisted stoutly, but the situation grew quickly untenable when the castle aqueduct was cut. In an act of celebrated heroism (or desperation) he then led a ferocious charge out of the castle and into the Rokkaku lines, causing them to flee. This episode, along with a series of other inspired victories, gained him the moniker *oni Shibata*, or "devil Shibata."

After Nobunaga's victory over the Asai and Asakura in 1573 he was given control of Echizen, and went to live at Kitanosho castle, from where he was planned a conquest of the Hokuriku *chiho*. After 1576, he pushed further north and into Kaga province to confront the *Ikko-ikki*. The campaign, fought with the assistance of Maeda Toshiie and Sassa Narimasa, proved to be both difficult and convoluted, although he eventually brought both Kaga and Noto to heel. He fought with Nobunaga against Uesugi Kenshin at Tedorigawa in 1577, and seized an opportunity presented by Kenshin's untimely death to push far into Etchu.

On the occasion of Nobunaga's assassination at Honno-ji, Katsuiie was engaged on his master's service, facing Uesugi's army at the siege of Matsukura and thus prevented from returning to confront Akechi Mitsuhide at Yamasaki. At the council held in Kiyosu to determine Nobunaga's successor, Katsuiie was one of those who stood for Oda Nobutaka, against Toyotomi Hideyoshi. This decision proved to be his downfall. The Shibata army, under the leadership of Sakuma Morimasa, was destroyed by Toyotomi Hideyoshi at Shizugatake in May 1583. Shortly after, Katsuiie retreated to Kitanosho where he set the fire to the castle and committed *seppuku*.

**Below:** Hideyoshi and Shibata Katsuie. The pair clashed over the question as to who should succeed Oda Nobunaga (the obvious successor, his eldest son had already been killed). Open warfare erupted with Shibata the eventual loser. *via Clive Sinclaire*

## Shimazu Iehisa
### (1547–1587)
#### Sengoku era military commander

Shimazu Iehisa was a Sengoku era military commander who distinguished himself in a number of battles fought on Kyushu. His family, the Shimazu was descended from Tadahisa, who from 1187 was military commander of southern Kyushu under Minamoto Yoritomo. Iehisa was the fourth son of Shimazu Takahisa; his elder half-brother Yoshihisa, for whom he fought numerous battles, was *daimyo* of the clan.

After many years of fighting their rivals in Hyuga, the clan was in a position to challenge the dominant Otomo. In 1578 Otomo Yoshimune and his father Sorin invaded Hyuga, sending an advance force under Tawara Chikataka to attack Iehisa at Takajo, a border fortress he was charged with guarding. Iehisa's 1,000-strong force resisted fiercely, allowing Yoshihisa time to gather men and advance north to confront the Otomo army. On December 10, the two sides clashed at the Mimigawa, a short distance from Taka castle. Despite repeated attacks by the Otomo army, Yoshihisa's battered lines held firm. He then led a counterattack, coordinated with Iehisa's move out of the

**Left:** Shimazu Iehisa battles on through the pouring rain. Many experts consider that he was the best leader and commander of the Shimazu clan of the entire Sengoku era.
*British Museum/Jo St Mart*

castle and into the enemy's rear, and scored a remarkable victory.

Iehisa went on to other glories, notably at the battle of Okitanawate (Hizen) in May 1584, where he engineered the victory of a Shimazu/Arima force over Ryuzoji Takanobu. His last action came during Hideyoshi's Kyushu campaign in 1587 when he fought to hold back the invaders. The clan was forced to surrender in mid-June, shortly before Iehisa died at Sadowara castle.

# Shimazu Yoshihisa
**(1533–1611)**
**Satsuma Province** *daimyo*

Shimazu Yoshihisa was a *daimyo* of Satsuma Province in the late Sengoku and early Edo periods, leader of the clan in some of its greatest victories. As the eldest son of Shimazu Takahisa, he succeeded as the head of Shimazu clan in 1566. He then embarked on an ambitious program to consolidate his power over Satsuma and Omi, and then to unify all of Kyushu under Shimazu control. By 1572 he had secured Satsuma, and in that year fought the first battle with his greatest rival, Ito Yoshisuke, at the battle of Kigasakihara. Victory at Kigasakihara enabled Yoshihisa to expand into Hyuga, defeating the Ito again at Takabaru in 1576.

In January 1578, Yoshihisa won a decisive encounter with Yoshisuke at Kamiya, and thereafter the Ito ceased to a threat. At the end of the year, Yoshihisa crushed an attempt by the Otomo to check him at the battle of

Mimigawa. With the victory over the Ryuzoji clan in 1584, the Shimazu could lay claim to most of Kyushu, and the Shimazu appeared to be on the cusp of realizing his dream of unification.

Those dreams were quickly shattered when in 1587 Toyotomi Hideyoshi sent an enormous host of 200,000 men on a campaign to bring Kyushu into line. In the face of overwhelming odds, the Shimazu were quickly driven back to Satsuma Province, where Yoshihisa surrendered in June 1587. Although most of the lands they had conquered were taken away, the Shimazu clan was allowed to hold on to Satsuma and Osumi provinces. Yoshihisa lived out the rest of his life as a Buddhist monk, handing stewardship of the clan to his brother Yoshihiro rule. He died of an illness in 1611.

## So Yoshitomo
**(1568–1615)**
*Daimyo* of the So clan

So Yoshitoshi was *daimyo* of the So clan through the late Sengoku and early Edo periods, and played a central role in Toyotomi Hideyoshi's Korean campaigns. His domain was Tsushima, the group of islands lying of the northwest coast of southern Honshu, and an important staging post between Japan and the continent.

In 1580, Tsushima was conquered in advance of Toyotomi Hideyoshi's Kyushu campaign. Yoshitoshi succeeded his father Yoshishige as head of the family, and became one of Toyotomi's trusted inner circle of retainers. Because of his well-established relations with and knowledge of Korea, Yoshotoshi acted as Hideyoshi's representative in negotiations with the Korean king, seeking to win passage for Japanese troops through Korea to China. Ultimately, his efforts came to nothing. In the subsequent invasions, fighting under Konishi Yukinaga, Yoshotoshi distinguished himself at the siege of Pusan (April 1592), and a number of ensuing engagements.

Later, during the decisive Sekigahara campaign, Yoshitoshi stood for Tokugawa Ieyasu but was not present in the decisive battle. Under the Ieyasu's new administration (the Tokugawa shogunate), Yoshitomo worked to rebuild relations with Korea. Yoshitomo died in 1615, but members of his clan served loyally as the *shogun*'s representatives to Korea for the next 250 years.

**Left:** Shimazu Yoshihisa was probably the greatest sixteenth century Kyushu general, although he was lucky to have the martial skills of the Satsuma warriors at his command and the outstanding military abilities of his brothers to help him. *British Museum/Jo St Mart*

**Right:** Statue of So Yoshitomo. via *jo stmart*

## Sue Harukata
### (1521–1555)
**Middle Sengoku era *daimyo***

Sue Harukata was a *daimyo* with land holdings in the western provinces of Japan during the mid-Sengoku era. His family were senior retainers of the Ouchi clan and his father was Sue Okifusa, who had distinguished himself as one of their military commanders.

In his youth Harukata befriended and later served Ouchi Yoshitaka. At the age of eighteen his father Okifusa died and he became the head of the Sue clan. From 1540 he conducted Ouchi Yoshitaka's campaign against the Amago clan and led the relief of Koriyama castle in 1540. The next year he was with Yoshitaka for a drive into Izumo, but the advance of the allied Ouchi/Mori army broke down in front of Gassan-Toda and thereafter Yoshitaka's interest in prosecuting the war faded. More ambitious elements

**Above:** Sue Harukata (center left) in battle. In the Western provinces he was known as *Saigoku-muso no Samuraidaisho* ("Samurai general without peer"). *British Museum/Jo St Mart*

within the Ouchi camp, led by Harukata and Otomo Sorin, began plotting and in 1551, staged a coup in which Yoshitaka was forced to commit suicide. The following year Harukata installed his adopted son Yoshinaga as the head of the clan.

Yoshinaga soon embarked on a

campaign of expansion, bringing conflict with other retainers of the Ouchi clan. In 1554 an alliance led by Yoshimi Masayori, and Mori Motonari rose against the Ouchi and in June defeated Harukata at the Oshikibata (in Aki). The next year, in October, Harukata was decisively beaten in an engagement on the sacred island of Miyajima, and committed suicide.

# Taira Kiyomori
## (1118–1181)
### Leader of the Taira clan

Taira no Kiyomori was leader of the Taira clan during the late Heian Period of Japan. His victory in the Genpei Wars of 1180–1185 led to the establishment of the first samurai-dominated administrative government in Japan. He is the main character in the Kamakura Period epic, the "Tale of Heike."

The Taira could trace their lineage back to Emperor Kammu, who had first bestowed the name on some of his grandsons. By the time of Kiyomori's birth the Taira was one of the four most powerful clans in Japan (the others were, in order of importance, Fujiwara, Minamoto, and Tachibana).

In 1153 Taira no Tadamori died, to be succeeded as leader of the clan by his son Kiyomori. Kiyomori wasted little time in finding ways to increase his personal power and influence. In 1156, a ripe opportunity for advancement presented itself, when he and Minamoto no Yoshitomo, head of the Minamoto clan, were called on to suppress the *Hogen no ran* (Hogen Rebellion). Three years later, the erstwhile allies had become bitter rivals, culminating in an attempt by Kiyomori's rivals (led by Minamoto no Yoshitomo) to effect an uprising. Kiyomori swiftly put down the Heiji Rebellion; Yoshitomo and his two eldest sons were killed, but he was persuaded to reprieve the three youngest, Yoritomo, Noriyori, and Yoshitsune. It was a decision he would live to regret.

Through the patronage of the retired sovereign, Go-Shirakawa, Kiyomori climbed high through the ranks of government, ultimately to the position (in 1167) of *Daijo-Daijin*, the chief minister of government. From this position he was able to manipulate the affairs of the court, and steadily brought about the resignation of his rivals from all government posts in 1179. In their place he put his allies and relatives. At the same time he imprisoned his former sponsor, the cloistered Emperor Go-Shirakawa. Then, in 1180 Kiyomori forced the emperor Takakura off the throne and put his grandson Prince Tokuhito (Emperor Antoku) in his place.

Kiyomori's abuses of power impelled many both within and outside the clan to turn against him. In the early summer of 1180, the Minamoto clan rose against the Taira sparking off the Genpei Wars. Kiyomori died early in the next year, and was thus spared from witnessing the destruction of his clan at Dan-no-Ura in 1185.

**Left:** Taira no Kiyomori was a successful politician and general. He is also the principal character in the *Tale of Heike*, the great Kamakura period epic set against the backdrop of the Genpei Wars. *jo stmart*

## Taira Koremori
**(1160–1184)**
**Military commander in the Genpei Wars**

Taira no Koremori was military commander during the late Heian period, and a significant figure in the Genpei Wars of that time. His first significant action came at Fujigawa in November 1180, where he attempted to halt the advance of Minamoto no Yoritomo into Suruga. At the pivotal battle of Kurikara in June 1183, he was outsmarted by Minamoto no Yoshinaka

扇宮実盛
手塚光盛　大奮戦之圖

て不足なしいざ参れ」光盛馬上より斬り込めば、滋籐の弓で受

く戦場に立ちたるならんとて其の勇を賞揚した。

in the famous action at the Kurikara Pass, on Mount Tonami in Etchu. This loss led directly to the abandonment of Kyoto, and the westward retreat of the Taira. Koremori's final action was at the naval battle at Ichinotani in March 1184, where the Taira were dealt another blow by Minamoto no Yoshitsune. Koremori escaped but committed suicide the following month.

**Left:** Kumagai no Jiro Naozane was a retainer of the Minamoto clan during the Genpei Wars. *Burstein Collection/Corbis*

**Above:** Taira Koremori fights Minamoto. Koremori. Taira Koremori was a Taira clan commander during the Genpei War. However, he lost both the battle of Fujigawa (1180) and the battle of Kurikara (1184) before he fled the field at the battle of Yashima. *via Clive Sinclaire*

# Taira no Masakado

## (d. 940)
### First *daimyo* and important member of the Taira clan

Taira no Masakado was a prominent member of the Taira clan during the early Heian era, remembered for his rebellion against the central government. Some scholars consider him to be the first *daimyo*.

Masakado was the son of Taira no Yoshimasa, *chinjufu-shogun* in the north of Japan. Masakado himself held lands in the Kanto region, and was a vassal of the Fujiwara. Refused a post in the government, in 935 he fomented a rebellion by attacking a government outpost in Hitachi Province, and killed the governor, his uncle Taira no Kunika. The revolt quickly spread, and in December he conquered Shimotsuke and Kozuke provinces, whereupon he claimed the title of *shinno* (new emperor). Masakado persuaded Fujiwara Sumitomo to join the rebellion, and in response the central government in Kyoto responded by sending an army commanded by Fujiwara no Hidesato and Taira no Sadamori, the son of Kunika, to quash the uprising. Masakado was brought to battle at Kojima (Shimousa) in 940 and defeated. His head and that of his coconspirator were displayed in the capital as a warning to any prospective rebels. The *Shomonki* ("Chronicle of Masakado") deals with the great disorders in the Kanto, which erupted into full-scale rebellion in the 930s under Masakado, written more than a 150 years after he died.

**Below and Right:** The final battle of Taira no Masakado. He had rebelled against the government, which made him a hero to local peoples, but after a price was put on his head he was killed by his cousin Sadamori and Fujiwara no Hidesato at the battle of Kojima. *via Clive Sinclaire (below) and British Museum/Jo St Mart*

# Taira Munemori
**(1147–1185)**
**Head of the Taira clan**

Taira Munemori was head of the Taira clan during the late Heian era, and the principal commander of the Taira forces during the Genpei Wars. When Munemori assumed leadership of the clan in 1181, following the death of his father Kiyomori, the Genpei Wars had entered a temporary hiatus brought on by a widespread famine. In the opening actions neither side had demonstrated that it had the upper hand. Both Minamoto and Taira had scored victories, and the outcome appeared to hang in the balance

In 1183, conditions had improved sufficiently for Munemori to send his son Koremori and brother Michimori in to Echizen against Minamoto Yoshinaka. However, the inexperienced Taira army was comprehensively beaten at the battle of Kurikara (June 1183), and Yoshinaka now advanced on Kyoto, precipitating a flight from the capital by Munemori with the emperor and royal family in tow. Munemori retreated to the west holding a forward base at Ichi-no-tani in Settsu, should an opportunity for a counter-attack present itself. However, in March 1184, Ichi-no-tani was attacked and taken by Minamoto Yoshitsune, eliminating the last line of defense to the western provinces.

The Minamoto launched a double-headed assault, moving west through Honshu, while Yoshitsune prepared for an assault on Yashima (Sanuki Province), Munemori's fortress on Shikoku and temporary home of the Imperial Court. Yashima was taken in March 1185 and Munemori forced back onto their base at Hikoshima in the

Shimonoseki Strait. With his back to the sea, and nowhere else to run, Munemori was forced to meet the Minamoto head-on. Outnumbered both in men and ships, his situation looked bleak.

On the morning of April 25, two mighty fleets collided at Dan-no-ura, off the southern tip of Honshu. Although initially the battle seemed to be swinging in his favor, Munemori was stung at a crucial juncture by a change in tidal conditions and defection of Taguchi Shigeyoshi to the Minamoto. Together these events sealed the battle. Almost of the Taira commanders drowned themselves. Munemori baulked at this and was later plucked out of the water by the Minamoto. He was escorted to Kyoto and executed later in 1185.

**Left:** Taira Munemori, although the leader of the clan, was one of the very few Taira not to commit *seppuku* after their humiliating defeat at the battle of Dan-no-ura in 1185. He was later captured and executed in Kyoto as a completely shamed man. *British Museum/Jo St Mart*

**Below :** Taira Shigemori and Fujiwara Nobuyori clash in combat during the *Heiji no ran* rebellion (August 1156). *via Clive Sinclaire*

# Taira Shigemori
## (1138–1179)
### Late Heian era court official and military commander

Taira no Shigemori was a late Heian era court official and military commander, and a key figure in both the *Hogen no ran* (Hogen rebellion) and subsequent *Heiji no ran* (Heiji rebellion). Shigemori was the eldest son Taira no Kiyomori

At the time of the outbreak of the *Hogen no ran* in August 1156, Shigemori was an official with the Ministry of Central Affairs. During the subsequent *Heiji no ran* Shigemori led cavalry against Minamoto no Yoshitomo and Fujiwara no Nobuyori, who were barricaded in the Shirakawa-den (Imperial Palace). After a fierce battle the occupants were driven out.

Shigemori lived for twenty more years before dying in 1179. He was a popular and talented leader, and many have pondered how things might have gone for the Taira had Shigemori succeeded instead of the much less capable Munemori.

# Taira Tomomori
## (1152–1185)
### Military commander in the Genpei Wars

Taira no Tomomori was a late Heian era military commander in the Genpei Wars, perhaps the best Taira general of that time. After defeating the combined forces of Minamoto Yorimasa and the warrior monks of the Miidera at the battle of Uji River in late June 1180, in April of the next year he defeated Minamoto no Yukiie at battle of Sunomatagawa in Owari, and then pursued him to the Yahagi River. In the ensuing battle he again put the enemy to flight but was taken ill forced to call off the chase. Tomomori won the naval action off Mizushima in 1183, but could not prevent the rout of the Taira fleet at Dan-no-Ura in 1185. Faced with imminent defeat, Tomomori reportedly tied himself to an anchor and threw himself off his ship.

**Left:** Dramatic print of Taira Shigemori and his magnificent horse. Shigemori took part in the Hogen and Heiji rebellions. *British Museum/Jo St Mart*

**Right:** A detail from the Ujigawa Kassen screen. © *Sakamoto Photo Research Laboratory/Corbis*

# Tajihi Agatamori
### (668–737)
### First *shogun*

Taira no Tomomori was a late Heian era military commander in the Genpei Wars, perhaps the best Taira general of that time. After defeating the combined forces of Minamoto Yorimasa and the warrior monks of the Mii-dera at the battle of Uji River in late June 1180, in April of the next year he defeated Minamoto no Yukiie at battle of Sunomatagawa in Owari, and then pursued him to the Yahagi River. In the ensuing battle he again put the enemy to flight but was taken ill and forced to call off the chase. Tomomori was again the victor at the naval action off Mizushima in 1183, but could not prevent the rout of the Taira fleet at Dan-no-Ura in 1185. Faced with imminent defeat, Tomomori reportedly tied himself to an anchor and threw himself off his ship.

**Right:** Although an important general Takeda Nobushige was killed at the Fourth battle of Kawanakajima (1561), fighting samurai belonging to Uesugi general Kakizaki Kageie. His head was recovered by Yamadera Nobuaki, a Takeda family retainer, who was also said to have killed his master's killer. Nobushige's body and head were buried at Kawanakajima, where his grave can still be seen. *British Museum/Jo St Mart*

**Far right:** Takeda Nobutora (left) at the battle of Un no Kuchi where his son, Takeda Harunobu later Shingen, won his first victory. *British Museum/Jo St Mart*

# Takeda Nobushige
## (d. 1561)
### Sengoku era military commander

Takeda Nobushige was a Sengoku era military commander in the service of his elder brother Takeda Shingen. Nobushige was famed for his knowledge of warfare and wise counsel. He was favored to inherit leadership of the clan by his father Nobutora, until his elder brother Harunobu (Shingen) rebelled and seized power for himself. Nonetheless, Nobushige accepted his brother as chief and fought alongside him in many encounters.

When Fujisawa Yorichika rose up in rebellion in 1544, Nobushige was ordered to undertake a retaliatory mission to capture Yorichika's Kojinyama castle. Two years later he and his nephew Yoshinobu captured Katsurao castle, the main castle of Murakami Yoshikiyo. He died at Kawanakajima in 1561.

# Takeda Nobutora
## (1493–1574)
### Sengoku era *daimyo*

Takeda Nobutora was a *daimyo* of Kai Province during the Sengoku era, and fought in a number of battles of the period. His Takeda clan was established in the eleventh century by Yoshikiyo, a retainer of Minamoto Yoshiie, and had already ruled Kai for over 300 years when Nobutora succeeded in 1507.

Soon after he faced challenges too

from the Hojo, Imagawa, and Uesugi, and then from his uncle, Takeda Nobue. He successfully resisted all of them and by 1519 had subjugated all of Kai. Over the course of the next decade he fought successfully to defend Kai against incursions by Fukushima Masashige in 1521 and Hojo Ujitsuna in 1526. His last major military action came in 1536, when he besieged Hiraga Genshin at Unnokuchi. Although he was forced to retreat, his son Harunobu (Shingen) eventually defeated Hiraga and took the castle. A successful military leader, Nobutora's heavy-handed administration of Kai made him an unpopular leader. When he expressed a desire for his son Nobushige to succeed, Harunobu overthrew his father and sent him into exile in Suruga. He died in March 1574, in Shinano.

**Above:** Statue of Takeda Shingen at Kofu station, Yamanashi. *wikipedia.com via Jo St Mart*
**Right:** Portrait of Takeda Shingen. *wikipedia.com via Jo St Mart*

# Takeda Shingen
## (1521–1573)
### Sengoku era *daimyo*

Takeda Shingen was one of the foremost Sengoku era daimyo, ruler over Shinano and Kai provinces, and winner of many victories as a military leader.

Shingen was the eldest son of Takeda Nobutora. His father evidently favored his younger brother, Nobushige, to succeed as clan leader, leading Shingen to wrest control in a July 1541 coup and send his father into exile with the Imagawa clan.

Shingen faced an abrupt threat by a coalition of *daimyo*s in the Shinano region against Kai Province. However, he caught them unprepared at the battle of Sezawa in April 1542 and scored a quick victory, facilitating an expansive drive into southern Shinano. He took the Suwa clan fortresses at Uehara and Kuwabara before moving on the Tozawa and Takato family in central Shinano Takato Yoritsugu.

Over the course of the next four years he won a remarkable series of victories in his bid to conquer Shinano, but in February 1548, he was temporarily checked by Murakami Yoshikiyo in a hotly contested battle at Uedahara, in which he was personally wounded and several top commanders killed. Shingen quickly recovered and continued his relentless campaign, eventually bottling up Murakami forces at Toishi castle. The Takeda general Sanada Yukitaka brought down the castle in 1551 and forced the defenders to surrender.

With much of Shinano now under his control, he now faced off the man who would emerge as his greatest rival, Uesugi Kenshin of Echigo. Between 1553 and 1561 Shingen (the so-called "Tiger of Kai") and Kenshin (who had the moniker "Dragon of Echigo") fought five times at the battles of Kawanakajima. Although costly, ultimately none of these battles was decisive.

By 1564, Shingen had completely subjugated Shinano Province, and thereafter made limited forays into Kozuke and Musashi, where he took several important castles. Beginning in 1568 he launched a concerted campaign against the Hojo in Sagami and Suruga, besieging their castles at Odawara, Mimasetoge Kanbara, and Fukazawa, coupled with attacks on the Imagawa Ujizane in Suruga.

By 1570, Shingen alone had the strength and ability to challenge Oda Nobunaga's in his relentless subjugation of Japan. After crushing the Imagawa, in November 1572 Shingen led an army into the domain of emergent threat Tokugawa Ieyasu, a Nobunaga ally. He captured Futamata, and then struck again in January 1573 at the battle of Mikatagahara, where he scored a minor victory over an allied Oda Nobunaga army. In spring, preparing to carry the battle further into Mikawa, he died at camp. Upon hearing of Shingen's death, Uesugi Kenshin reportedly broke into tears.

Shingen's death was a irreplaceable loss to the Takeda. Two years later, at Nagashino, Ieyasu and Nobunaga dealt a crushing blow to the weakened clan from which it never recovered. Many of governmental and military institutions of the Tokugawa shognunate were in fact borrowed from Shingen.

**Right:** Tokugawa Ieyasu (center left) at the battle of Sekigahara in 1600. *British Museum/Jo St Mart*

**Below:** In a surprise attack during the fourth Kawakanajima battle in 1561, Uesuji Kenshin attacks Takeda Shingen who defends himself with his *Gumpai-wichiwa* (fan). *via Clive Sinclaire*

# Tokugawa Ieyasu
(1543–1616)
**Founder and first** *shogun* **of the Tokugawa Shogunate**

Tokugawa Ieyasu was the founder and first *shogun* of the Tokugawa Shogunate that ruled from 1600 until the Meiji Restoration in 1868. He completed the process of unification started by Oda Nobunaga and his rival Toyotomi Hideyoshi, and is often heralded as the finest samurai leader of all.

Tokugawa Ieyasu was born in Mikawa Province, the son of Matsudaira Hirotada, *daimyo* of Mikawa, and was given the name Matsudaira Takechiyo. At this time the Matsudaira clan was divided into two factions, one of which favored the Imagawa clan; the other side stood for the Oda. In his youth, Ieyasu witnessed the bitter struggles that resulted from this family feud.

Under Nobuhide, the Oda made frequent attempts to expand into Mikawa while Takechiyo was still an infant. In 1547, Nobuhide invaded Mikawa again prompt Hirotada to issue an appeal for help to his ally Imagawa Yoshimoto. Yoshimoto assented to help, on condition that Hirotada send his son Takechiyo to him as "security."

However, as Takechiyo was being conveyed to a new life in bondage, a column of Nobuhide's men intercepted his retinue, and took Takechiyo captive. Nobuhide pressed Hirotada to sever his alliance with the Imagawa clan, threatening to execute his hostage unless he complied. Hirotada refused, but his son was spared to live in captivity at the Manshoji Temple in Nagoya.

In 1549, both Hirotada and Nobuhide died and Takechiyo found

himself used as a bargaining tool in a brokered deal between Oda Nobunaga and the Imagawa clan. Takechiyo was taken to the Imagawa's Sumpu castle, where he lived until he was fifteen.

After twelve years away from his homeland, he was allowed to return to his native Mikawa. Subsequently, he fought for the Imagawa against the Oda, achieving a minor victory at the siege of Terabe in 1558.

In May 1560 he was with Imagawa Yoshimoto for the march on Kyoto. During the advance, Motoyasu was dispatched to seize a fort at Marune. The fort was quickly taken and, perhaps fortuitously, he was guarding it when Yoshimoto's army was thoroughly routed at Okehazama in Owari.

Yoshimoto's death at Okezahama presented Ieyasu (as he was now called) with an opportunity to cut his nominal ties to the Imagawa. He now shifted his allegiance to Oda Nobunaga, through a secretly agreed deal, and in 1561, gave an open declaration of his loyalties by capturing the Imagawa fortress of Kaminojo. His wife and son were bartered for the wife and daughter of Udono Nagamachi, the castellan.

In the course of the early 1560s Ieyasu set about pacifying Mikawa, during which time he defeated the unruly *monto* within Mikawa province. In 1567, he took the name Ieysau Tokugawa, and the following year was with Oda Nobunaga on his march to Kyoto.

Meanwhile Ieyasu steadily expanded his own domain, arranging

**Far left:** Tokugawa Ieyasu was renouned for taking the heads of his opponents. *via CS*
**Left:** Englishman William Adams, the inspiration for James Clavell's John Blackthorne, traveled to Japan and became an advisor to Tokugawa Ieyasu, building western-style ships for him. *Bettmann/Corbis*

titanic struggle at Nagashino in 1575, where Nobunaga and Ieyasu dealt a crucial blow to Takeda Katsuyori and his clan's ambitions.

In May 1582 the Takeda were finally vanquished when a combined Oda-Tokugawa force attacked and conquered Kai and Shinano. That June, Ieyasu learned of Nobunaga's shock death and quickly assembled his army; in the event he was too late to take a part in the action at Yamazaki where Akechi Mitsuhide was killed.

In the disorder that followed, Ieyasu absorbed Kai and Shinano. Hojo Ujimasa responded to this by advancing into the two provinces, but the two reached a peaceful compromise that left Ieyasu in as master of Kai and Shinano provinces, while the Hojo took control of Kozuke Province.

In 1584, in the dispute over Nobunaga's successor, Ieyasu threw in his lot with Oda Nobukatsu, the eldest son and heir of Oda Nobunaga, against Hideyoshi. In the resulting Komaki Campaign, Hideyoshi led an army into Owari, only to be defeated at Nagakute and forced to withdraw in the middle of the year. Months of maneuvering and feints followed, and in January the war was settled through negotiation.

These events seem to have bred

a deal with Takeda Shingen to conquer and divide Imagawa lands between them. In 1570, Ieyasu's troops captured Totomi Province while Shingen's troops captured Suruga Province. This brief alliance was broken when Ieyasu gave sanctuary to their erstwhile enemy, Imagawa Ujizane, and he subsequently formed a pact with Uesugi Kenshin, Shingen's foremost opponent. In May he joined Nobunaga for an attack on the Asakura in Echizen and Omi, and in July Ieyasu helped to defeat both the Azai and Asakura clans at the battle of Anegawa.

In October 1571, Takeda Shingen attacked Totomi, igniting seven years of conflict between Ieyasu and the Takeda, the focus of which was the

some mistrust of Ieyasu in Hideyoshi's camp, as he was not called on to participate in the invasion of Shikoku, or the Kyushu campaigns.

In 1590 Hideyoshi moved against his last significant obstacle, the Hojo, who continued to rule defiantly over Kanto region. Ieyasu, a nominal ally of Hojo Ujimasa, committed his samurai to the vast host Hideyoshi assembled for the campaign. After crossing over into Sagami, they together laid siege to the Hojo bastion of Odawara castle. Sometime during this siege, with victory imminent, Hideyoshi made a surprising offer, pledging the eight Kanto provinces in return for Ieyasu's current domain.

After some consideration, Ieyasu accepted the deal, a decision that later was to have major ramifications.

After the surrender of the Hojo in August, Ieyasu moved his retinue to the Kanto region, taking Edo castle as his personal residence. Over the next decade he consolidated his position in the Kanto, and grew strong, rising to become the second most powerful *daimyo* in Japan.

Ieyasu's troops took no part in the Korean campaign, although he himself was called to Hideyoshi's court in Nagoya (Kyushu) to serve as a military advisor. He stayed there, off and on for the next five years. In 1598, Ieysau was made one of the *go-tairo*

(the council of five elders) who were to act as regents to his young son Hideyori after Hideyoshi's death. Among these five men Ieyasu was clearly the strongest. Shortly after Hideyoshi died; although Hideyori was now *shogun*, the go-tairo was the real power behind the throne.

However, the go-tairo soon split into two factions, one driven by the resurgent ambitions of Tokugawa Ieyasu, and the other by those who opposed him, led by the Toyotomi clan bureaucrat Ishida Mitsunari. The rival factions continued their feuding for two years, with each independently ambitious of creating an all-powerful new shogunate, until the fragile peace was finally broken and Ieyasu and Mitsunari faced up to each other on the battlefield, at what is now Sekigahara, in Gifu.

Ishida Mitsunari's claim to support the interests of Hideyoshi's son and elected heir, Hideyori, attracted many former Toyotomi allies to his side, and this despite his relative lack of experience on the battlefield. He was thus able to call on the support of many clans of the recent past, such the Mori of Choshu, the Kobayakawa, the Kikkawa, the Ukita and the Shimazu of Satsuma, and bring an army of some 80,000 to Sekigahara. As most of these families had their power-base in western Japan, Ishida's forces are generally referred to as the "Army of the West."

Ieyasu, by then the most powerful individual on the council and with a distinguished military career behind him, was considerably better versed in matters of war than his rival. Supported by his family, the Matsudaira, and capable generals such as Ii Naomasa, Ieyasu had also been successful in gaining the alliance of some notable *daimyo* families including the Kato, the Hosokawa, and the Kuroda. Collectively referred to as the "Army of the East," (as they were mostly based was in the eastern provinces) together they numbered some 74,000.

The battle at Sekigahara was the biggest and likely the most important

**Above left:** Samurai approaching a castle rebuilt by Ieyasu on the Tokaido Road. *The Art Archive/Tokyo University/Laurie Platt Winfrey*
**Right:** A portrait of Tokugawa Ieyasu from Japanese popular print. *The Art Archive*

battle in Japanese history. It began on October 21 and ended with a complete Tokugawa victory. The Army of the West was crushed and most of its leaders including Ishida Mitsunari captured and killed. Those that remained were forced to sign an oath of fealty to him. In everything but name Tokugawa Ieyasu was now the ruler of all Japan.

In 1603, Tokugawa Ieyasu received the title of *shogun* from Emperor Go-Yozei. Ieyasu was by now sixty years old, and he spent his remaining life creating and solidifying the Tokugawa Shogunate. Among the many projects that he undertook were the building of Edo castle, and the remodeling of the imperial court and buildings in Kyoto. Starting in 1609, he began efforts to isolate Japan from European influence, culminating in 1614, with the Christian Expulsion Edict, which banned Christianity, expelled all Christians and foreigners. Around that time, he instituted a law that severely limited the powers of the *daimyo*.

In 1615 he faced off a final challenge to his authority by Toyotomi Hideyori, and defeated him at the siege of Osaka castle. In 1616, at age seventy-five, Ieyasu died. The shogunate he established survived him by 250 years, standing as testimony to the remarkable achievements of a remarkable man.

## Torii Mototada
### (1539–1600)
### Later Sengoku era *daimyo*

Torii Mototada was a *daimyo*, and military commander under Tokugawa Ieyasu, during the later Sengoku era. He is lionized for a heroic act of self-sacrifice at the siege of Fushimi.

Mototada was the son of Torii Tadayoshi, a vassal of Matsudiara Hirotada and administrator for Tokugawa Ieyasu. In his youth Mototada was held as a hostage with Ieyasu by the Imagawa, and subsequently entered his service. He was at Mikatagahara and at Nagashino, where Oda Nobunaga crucified another clan member, Torii Suneemon. He fought against Sanada Masayuki in Shinano and later in the Odwara campaign, for which he was given a modest fief in Shimosa.

In the prologue to the Battle of Sekigahara, Mototada was ordered to hold Fushimi castle, in Kyoto. In August 1600, a 40,000-strong Toyotomi army led by Ishida Mitsunari marched on to Fushimi. Realizing that he stood little chance of resisting this mighty force, Mototada nevertheless chose to make a stand, proclaiming in a final letter to his son:

*"It is not the Way of the Warrior to be shamed and avoid death even under circumstances that are not particularly important . . . For myself, I am resolved to make a stand within the castle and to die a quick death. It would not take much trouble to break through a part of their numbers and escape, no matter how many tens of thousands of horsemen approached for the attack or by how many columns we were surrounded. But that is not the true meaning of being a warrior, and it would be difficult to account as loyalty. Rather, I will stand off the forces of the entire country here, and . . . die a resplendent death."*

Mitsunari's army began their assault on August 27, but after ten days he had made little progress against the bastion. A message was then sent into the castle tied to an arrow, revealing that the besieging army had taken the wife and children of one of the defenders hostage, and that they would suffer crucifixion unless the man betrayed his fellow defenders. With little choice but to comply, on September 8, one of the towers was set aflame from within the castle, and a number of Ishida's men were able to penetrate the castle defenses. The central keep was then burned, but Torii and his garrison battled on, despite knowing of their inevitable defeat, until all but ten of them were still standing. Mototada then killed himself and his family, and the castle fell into Mitsunari's hands.

Nevertheless, by this supreme act of self-sacrifice Ishida Mitsunari's attention was diverted away from his Nakasendo fortresses, which were

**Left:** Torii Mototada on horseback with his retinue. *British Museum/Jo St Mart*

then attacked by Tokugawa. It thus served a crucial role in allowing for greater strategic victories for Tokugawa, and has ever since been hailed as a shining example of the samurai spirit.

## Toyotomi Hideyoshi
### (1537–1598)
### Sengoku era *daimyo*

Toyotomi Hideyoshi was a *daimyo* in the Sengoku era, who fostered the process of unification begun by Oda Nobunaga and effectively brought peace to Japan after more than a century of civil war.

Although Hideyoshi's life before 1570 is shrouded in mystery, his birthplace is generally given as Nakamura-ku, in Owari (present day Nagoya in Aichi prefecture) the domain of the Oda. His father, Yaemon, was a peasant farmer who was an *ashigaru* (foot soldier) in Oda Nobunaga's army, and like all members of his class had no surname. As a young man, Hideyoshi entered the service of Matsushita Kahei, a vassal of the Imagawa clan, and subsequently journeyed to Suruga where he served *daimyo* Imagawa Yoshimoto.

In 1557 (or thereabouts) he returned to Owari and joined Oda Nobunaga's retinue. As Nobunaga's sandal-bearer he was present at

Okehazama in 1560, which presaged his master's rise to become the preeminent warlord in the land. Thereafter Hideyoshi rose steadily through the staff hierarchy, entrusted with more important tasks. In 1564, when Nobunaga was seeking ways to weaken Saito Tatsuoki, Hideyoshi convinced a number of Mino warlords and Saito samurai to shift their allegiances and turn on their master. In 1567 Nobunaga marched in and took Tatsuoki's Inabayama castle (now Gifu castle), a success which may be partially attributed to Hideyoshi's efforts.

By 1570 Hideyoshi had risen to become one of Nobunaga's most important generals. That year he led troops against the Asai and Asakura in the battle of Anegawa and three years later, after the Azai and Asakura had been finally quashed, Nobunaga gifted him three districts in the northern part of Omi Province. Hideyoshi eventually established himself at Imahama on Lake Biwa, and began work on a castle. The peasant's son and former sandal-bearer was thus now *daimyo*.

Hideyoshi spent much of the 1570s campaigning for Nobunaga, fighting in the siege of Nagashima in 1573–1574 and against the Takeda at Nagashino in 1575. The following year as part of Nobunaga's efforts against the Ishiyama Honganji, Hideyoshi embarked on what proved to be a long and difficult campaign through the Chugoku region against the Mori clan. He took Himeji, Kozuki, and Sayo castles, but ran in to stiff opposition at Miki, a strategically vital link in the defense of the Ishiyama Honganji. Miki continued to resist all efforts to bring it down until finally surrendering in 1580. Progressing slowly west Hideyoshi secured Harima and in 1580 he dispatched a force north into Inaba and began a 200-day siege of Tottori, an important Mori stronghold.

In April 1582, Hideyoshi invested Takamatsu, another Mori fortress in

**Left:** Portrait of Toyotomi Hideyoshi. *British Museum/Jo St Mart*

**Below:** Toyotomi Hideyoshi, one of the greatest Samurai leaders, whose reign is named after his castle in Kyoto, Momoyama. *via Clive Sinclaire*

Bingo. He was engaged here in June, when news came through of Nobunaga's death at the Honno-ji. Hideyoshi quickly brokered at truce with the Mori and led his army off to confront the usurper, Akechi Mitsuhide. After a lightning march spanning three provinces, he caught up with Misuhide at Yamazaki, and swiftly defeated him.

In the succession dispute that followed, Hideyoshi dismissed the heir by default, Oda Nobutaka, in favor of Oda Hidenobu. This stance put him in direct opposition to Shibata Katsuie, and tension quickly escalated between the two. The following May

Hideyoshi destroyed Katsuie's forces at the battle of Shizugatake, and consolidated his own power by absorbing most of the Oda clan into his control. Also in 1583, Hideyoshi ordered construction of Osaka castle on the site of Ishiyama Honganji, recently destroyed by Nobunaga. The castle would become the last stronghold of the Toyotomi clan after Hideyoshi's death.

Meanwhile, the dispute over who should succeed Nobunaga dragged on, prompting Oda Nobukatsu to seek a resolution through an alliance with Tokugawa Ieyasu against Hideyoshi. In the resulting Komaki campaign of

1584, the two sides fought two inconclusive battles at Komaki and Nagakute, after which a stalemate quickly set in. A peace treaty was formally agreed the following year, removing the *raison d'être* for war between the Tokugawa and Toyotomi clans.

Hideyoshi, his military and political power now firmly in ascendence, began to covet the title of *shogun*, official recognition of his position as the tacit ruler of Japan. His entreaties met with rebuff and he finally settled instead for the position of *kampaku* (regent).

In early 1585, Hideyoshi subjugated

Kii Province, and in the early summer sent a huge army to bring Shikoku under control. He took control of Etchu Province in September and in February 1587 led an army to Kyushu, where he defeated the Shimazu clan at the decisive battle at Sendai River.

In August 1588, Hideyoshi ordered the so-called "Great Sword Hunt" a landmark edict that called for the confiscation of arms from the peasantry, and limited ownership to samurai. The measure effectively stopped peasant revolts, ensuring greater stability by preventing individual *daimyo* from raising armies. The defeat of the Hojo clan in Kanto

in 1590 eliminated the last coherent resistance to Hideyoshi's authority, and marked the end of the Sengoku Period.

Hideyoshi was now fifty-three years old, and the first signs of declining health began to appear. His ambition, however, still burned bright, and he sought after some accomplishment to solidify his legacy. Like his predecessor, Oda Nobunaga, Hideyoshi dreamed of conquering China, and this prompted him to launch two ambitious but fated invasions of the Korean peninsula, in 1592 and 1598.

Hideyoshi had begun communi-

cating with the Korean king in 1587, requesting unmolested passage into China. When this was refused, Hideyoshi ordered preparations for an invasion. The first wave of Japanese troops landed at Pusan in the spring of 1592 and initially they enjoyed much success. However, despite the

**Left:** Toyotomi Hideyoshi's first battle. *via Clive Sinclaire*

**Below:** Toyotomi Hideyoshi is said to have been born the son of a foot soldier—but is seen as a great hero who ushered in a golden age. *via Clive Sinclaire*

Japanese victories on land, the Korean navy proved themselves masters of the seas, and cut the vital supply lines. After a period of stalemate a cease-fire was agreed, and Japanese troops retreated to Japan.

After several years of negotiations Hideyoshi launched his second invasion of Korea in 1597, but this met with even less success against the combined Chinese/Korean armies. By June 1598, the campaign was stalled, and Hideyoshi gave tacit approval for a withdrawal. Though he had dreamed of conquering Ming China, Japanese forces had never got beyond the Korean peninsula.

In August, with his health in terminal decline, Hideyoshi established the *go-tairo* (council of five regents) to rule until his son came of age. It was his last act.

In September 1598, Hideyoshi finally succumbed to years of ill-health.

Hideyoshi's legacy can be seen in many aspects of Japanese society. Among other things, he introduced a rigid class structure, restrictions on travel between different provinces, and conducted surveys of land and production that formed the basis for systematic taxation. Hideyoshi also influenced the material culture of Japan, particularly his beloved tea ceremony. In the political sphere, he set up a governmental system that balanced out the most powerful *daimyo*. The intrinsic value of his work may be gauged by the fact that in establishing his shogunate Tokuagawa Ieyasu left in place the majority of Hideyoshi's decrees and institutions.

## Uesugi Kagekatsu
### (1556–1623)
**Sengoku/early Edo era *daimyo***

Uesugi Kagekatsu was *daimyo* and military commander during the later Sengoku and early Edo era, a key opponent of Tokugawa Ieyasu in the events that prefaced the epochal battle of Sekigahara. Kagekatsu was the son of Nagao Masakage, a one-time opponent of Uesugi Kenshin in Echigo. Masakage died in 1564, and the childless Kenshin took Kagekatsu as his son. Upon Kenshin's death fourteen years later in 1578, Kagekatsu fought against his brother (through adoption) Kagetora for the succession, in a dispute known as the *Otate no ran* (Otate Rebellion). Kagekatsu prevailed and in the summer of 1579 forced his brother to commit suicide.

The turmoil that afflicted the Uesugi during this time allowed Oda Nobunaga to march in and take most of their Hokuriku domain. In 1582, Kagekatsu attempted to confront Nobunaga in Etchu, but met with a defeat at the hands of Oda forces at the battle of Tenjinyama, and was quickly threatened by advances into his remaining lands in Echigo. After Nobunaga's death, Kagekatsu aligned

**Far left:** Hideyoshi blows his great war trumpet at dawn before his victory at Shizugatake, 1583. *Asian Art & Archaeology Inc./Corbis*

**Left:** Osaka Castle was built by Hideyoshi and has been restored to its original glory. Inside its grounds is a shrine to Hideyoshi

with Toyotomi Hideyoshi, and fought as one of his commanders at Shizugatake in 1583, in the Komaki campaign of 1584, and against Shibata Shigiie in Echigo in 1585.

He subsequently battled with the Hojo in Kozuke, and in the 1590 Odawara campaign. After serving in Korea in the 1590s Kagakatsu received a huge fief in Echigo, and rose to even greater heights with his appointment to become a member of the council of Five Elders.

However, after Hideyoshi's death in 1598 Kagekatsu chose to ally himself with Ishida Mitsunari, against Tokugawa Ieyasu. He then provided the catalyst for the revolt against Tokugawa Ieyasu by building a castle in Mutsu, in clear defiance of the Council, prompting Ieyasu to begin preparing for a punitive expedition against him. But Uesugi's plan to draw Tokugawa Ieyasu north, and thereby distract him from Ishida Mitsunari's attacks in and around Osaka, was easily sniffed out by his adversary, and he sat tight in Osaka to fight Ishida. Kagekatsu now began preparing to move on Ieyasu from the northeast, while Ishida attacked from the west. His plans were nipped in the bud when Ieyasu sent Mogami Yoshiaki and Date Masamune north and defeated Kagekatsu at the siege of Shiroishi castle.

In the aftermath of the battle at Sekigahara, Kagekatsu declared his allegiance to Tokugawa Ieyasu, and lived out his life as a *tozama* (outsider) *daimyo*, at his much reduced estate in Tohoku. He fought for the Tokugawa Shogunate against the Toyotomi clan in the 1614–1615 siege of Osaka, and died in 1623.

# Uesugi Kenshin
## (1530–1578)
### Important *daimyo* of the Sengoku era

Uesugi Kenshin was one of the most important *daimyo* of the Sengoku era, famed for his rivalry with Takeda Shingen and vaunted as one of the outstanding commanders of his age.

Kenshin was the fourth son of Nagao Tamekage, and was initially known as Kagetora. After Tamekage was killed in fighting against the *Ikko-ikki* in Etchu, a succession dispute erupted between Kenshin's brothers. The eldest Harukage, emerged as the victor and and Kenshin found himself relocated to Rizen temple, where he resided until 1544.

Harukage proved to an ineffective and unpopular ruler, and faced with the threat of the Hojo expansion in the Kanto region, some of his late father's retainers recognized the need for a unified clan and began to seek a way of removing Harukage from power. In 1554, by now a boy of fourteen, Kenshin was urged by the conspirators to challenge his older brother Harukage for rule. Once Kenshin was convinced of the perspicacity of this venture, he led troops in a series of engagements against his brother, eventually prevailing to wrest control of the clan in 1547.

Kenshin now set out to consolidate

**Below left:** Uesugi Kenshin during one of the Kawakanajima battles. *via Clive Sinclaire*
**Below:** Uesugi Kenshin in battle. *British Museum/Jo St Mart*

his power in the region and unify the clan, and had gained control of most of Echigo by 1551, but found these efforts stymied by the pressing need to meet the challenge of Takeda Shingen. Thus began a legendary rivalry, in which the two fought a series of epic but indecisive encounters at Kawanakajima. The fourth battle—the only one in which any real fighting took place—is remembered for an episode in which Kenshin engaged Shingen at his field headquarters. Kenshin was driven off, and his army forced to retreat.

Though the battles with Takeda Shingen at Kawanakajima are the most celebrated of Uesugi Kenshin's actions, he actually fought in many other significant encounters with Shingen and other warlords in which the outcome was more decisive. In September 1560, he launched a drive to retake control of the Kanto back from the Hojo, culminating in the siege of Odawara castle in Sagami Province in June of the following year. Over the course of the next eighteen years he would launch many more raids on the Hojo domain. At the end of the the year he took the Hojo bastion of Matsuyama castle at 1561, losing it again two years later to an allied Hojo/Takeda army. At this time he received the title of *Kanto-kanrei* from the *shogun*, Ashikaga Yoshiteru.

Throughout the 1560s Uesugi faced the persistent problems in Etchu, requiring his intervention in the province to subdue both the local *Ikko-ikki* bands and the Shiina and Jinbo clans. By 1576, Etchu was effectively under his control.

Although Uesugi's territorial ambitions were limited, it was perhaps inevitable that he would clash at some point with Oda Nobunaga. He then seized upon an opportunity to take land in Noto, a province in the Hokuriku region that both he and Nobunaga saw as within their nominal spheres. In response, Nobunaga sent Shibata Katsuie to confront him. Despite a major numerical disadvantage, in November 1577 Kenshin pulled off what was probably his greatest victory at the Tedorigawa, and forced Nobunaga to pull back to Omi Province while Kenshin contented himself with building a few forts in neighboring Kaga before returning to Echigo for the winter.

During the winter of 1577–1578, Uesugi Kenshin maded preparations for a major expedition against Nobunaga, but he was reportedly in very poor health. The following spring, on April 19, he died of complications that may have stemmed from his fondness for drink. Kenshin did not leave a legitimate male heir and upon his death his two adopted sons immediately entered into a long and ruinous power struggle, which weakened the clan considerably.

## Ukita Hidiie
### (1573–1655)
### Sengoku/Edo period *daimyo*

Ukita Hidiie was the *daimyo* of Bizen and Mimasaka provinces during the late Sengoku and Edo periods, one of Toyotomi Hideyoshi's foremost commanders and later one of the *go-tairo* (council of five regents).

Hidiie's father was the nominal Urakami family vassal Ukita Naoie, who had usurped his masters and come to rule over all of Bizen. After Naoie died in 1582, the young Hidiie was taken in and raised by Toyotomi Hideyoshi.

For the second Korean campaign, the nineteen-year-old Hidiie was chief field commander. He served as one of the five regents following Hideyoshi's death in 1598, and from Okayama castle ruled over over a substantial fief encompassing Bizen, Mimasaka, and part of Bitchu.

He took sides with Ishida Mitsunari in the prologue to the fighting in 1600 and brought a large army to the definitive battle at Sekigahara. Following the defeat of Mitsunari's army, Hidie found refuge with the Shimazu, but was betrayed in 1603 by Shimazu Iehisa. Condemned to die by Tokugawa Ieyasu, his sentence was reduced to exile. He died at the age of ninty on isolated Hachijo Island, part of the Izu islands lying south of Edo.

**Right**: Ukita Hidiie sided with Ishida Mitsunari and fought at Sekigahara. *British Museum/Jo St Mart*

時富戈の悴蝶三郎を妻小抱色浪花小赴きしに
星の閑居あれ六愛小便て潜小盟約の大儀を企ちけ
八主君小恩儀深く父諾を進く媒有て縁を結び
討ふ八せめて母の妄頼ありて身小狸ひ本望を
其夜八雪の翌日うる
表八蚤の如くありしが
かりける塩谷判官の家来
御首を申請小推参せり
小遠さを嘖き叫び合手八
る所小側より火鉢を
ど世澤の
る元来
真多や
素
小飛ばつ

一勇齋
國芳

## Yamagata Masakage
### (1524–1575)
### Sengoku era military commander

Yamagata Masakage was a military commander during the Sengoku era, famous for his distinctive profile and skill in battle. He was the younger brother of Obu Toramasa, one of the

most important and valued of Shingen's retainers, but Masakage is thought to have implicated his brother in a plot against Takeda Harunobu. As one of the so-called "Twenty-Four Generals" of the Takeda clan, Masakage led a highly effective and much feared cavalry unit that was dubbed the *furinkazan*, or "red fire unit," a name derived from the slogan on Shingen's personal war banner.

The *furinkazan* were outfitted in bright red armor, and reportedly opened any attack.

Masakage fought in a great number of Shingen's battles, for which he had a fief in Shinano as a reward. He was at Mimasetoge in 1569, the siege of Yoshida castle, and the following battle of Mikatagahara. His last battle was at Nagashino in 1575 where he fell to musket fire while charging at

the head of his famous unit. Later, Ii Naomasa adopted Yamagata's red color, and paid tribute to him by naming his army the "Red Devil Brigade."

**Left**: Portrait of Yamagate Masakage. *British Museum/Jo St Mart*

**Below**: Yamagate Masakage in battle. *British Museum/Jo St Mart*

# Yamana Sozen
## (1404–1473)
### Muromachi era *daimyo*

Yamana Sozen was a Muromachi era *daimyo*, and a bitter rival of Hosokawa Katsumoto during the Onin War in Kyoto.

The Yamana clan, whose domain was Inaba Province, could claim descent from Minamoto Yoshishige. They became powerful in the Muromachi period, predominantly through their support of the Ashikaga, but their fortunes had fluctuated since. Yamana Sozen, whose name was Michitoyo prior to accepting the tonsure of a Buddhist monk, grew envious of the greater influence of the Hosokawa, personified by his son-in-law Katsumoto. In 1464, Sozen used the pretext of a succession dispute over the shogunate to confront Katsumoto directly. Three years later, having spent the ensuing period in building their armies, the first skirmishes of the Onin War began. After several months of deadlock, in March of 1467 Sozen ignited the war by attacking and burning the mansion of a Hosokawa officer.

Widespread fighting then broke out, in the course of which much of Kyoto was destroyed. In early 1468, nearly a year since the war began, there was a let up in the fighting, followed by a interval of several years in which both men engaged each other in political, not military, conflict. A peaceful resolution was eventually agreed.

**Below:** "War is conducted at a run." One of a series of modern illustrations in the sequence "The Face of Battle" by R. Knutsen, this shows Muromachi or Sengoku *jidai* period troops. *via Clive Sinclaire*

# Chronology

| | |
|---|---|
| 660 B.C. | Jimmu Tenno (c.711.–c.585.B.C.) becomes Japan's first emperor and sets up the ruling Yamato State. Weaponry and armor start to be developed. |
| Fifth century A.D. | Horses first used in Japanese combat. |
| 538 | A Korean delegation introduces Buddhism to the Japanese emperor— it rapidly becomes a powerful philosophy for rulers and warriors. |
| 550 | Indigenous Japanese religion is named Shinto to differentiate it from Buddhism and Confucianism. |
| 600 | First official Japanese delegation is sent to China. |
| 604 | Start of the Japanese empire when Prince Shotoku issues the Kenpo *Jushichijo* (constitution) based on Confucian principles. |
| 605 | Buddhism and Confucianism become the dual state religions of Japan. |
| 645 | Start of the Asuka-Nara period as Kotoku Tenno introduces the Taika Reform, which strengthens imperial power over aristocratic clans, turning their states into provinces. |
| 702 | Taiho law codes establishes the Great Council of State. It also provides for the establishment of *kuni* (provinces) ruled by governors. |
| 710 | City of Nana replaces Asuka as the capital of Japan. |
| 781 | Emperor Kammu comes to power. |
| 784 | Emperor Kammu moves the capital to Nagaoka. |
| 794 | Start of the Heian period and the capital is moved again, this time to Kyoto (Heian-kyo). |
| 838 | The emperor forbids all contact with China. |
| 858 | Emperor Seiwa of the Fujiwara clan takes control of the imperial court. |
| 935 | Taira Masakado revolts in Kanto provinces and proclaims himself the new emperor. |
| 939 | Taira Masakado killed by Fujiwara no Hidesato. |
| c.1000 | Sei Shonagon writes *Pillow Book*. |
| 1051–63 | *Zenkunen kassen* (Early Nine-Years War) |
| 1062 | Battle of Kuriyagawa |
| 1068 | The Fujiwara clan are overthrown by Emperor Go-Sanjo. |
| 1087 | First of the *insei* (cloistered emperors) as Emperor Shirakawa abdicates to become a Buddhist monk. |
| 1156 | End of the *insei* era with the defeat of the Monomoto clan by Taira Kiyomori. |
| 1159–60 | Heiji conflict; Taira no Kiyomori gains military control of eastern Japan. |
| 1180 | Antoku, the eight-year-old grandson of Taira no Kiyomori is put on the throne. |
| 1180–85 | Minamoto Yoritomo takes up arms against the Heike (Taira) clan in the Genpei Wars. |
| 1185 | Battle of Dan-no-Ura; end of the Genpei Wars and start of the Kamakura period: Minamoto Yoritomo becomes the first *shogun* of Japan and the emperor is reduced to a figure-head. |

Samurai are now the leading noble class in Japan.

| | |
|---|---|
| 1185–1336 | Rule of the Minamoto family—the Kamakura *bakufu*. |
| 1192 | Minamoto Yoritomo becomes first permanent *shogun* of Japan and sets up his shogunate in Kamakura. The *bakufu* system of government starts. |
| 1199 | Minamoto Yoritomo dies. |
| 1219 | The last Minamoto *shogun*, Sanetomo is assasinated. |
| 1221 | Emperor Go-Toba tries to retake control of the country; samurai families led by Hojo Masako unite to defeat him. |
| 1232 | The *Joei shikimoku* (Kamakura Law Code) is issued by the Hojo. |
| Late 1200s | Mongols invade Japan. |
| 1274 | First Mongol invasion as Kublai Khan and his hordes attempt to invade Japan but are repelled by the *kamikaze*. The samurai begin to adopt a style of formation combat. |
| 1281 | Second Mongol invasion attempt. |
| 1318 | Go-Daigo becomes the 96th Emperor of Japan. He later attempts to over-throw the Hojo regents, giving rise instead to a new dynasty of *shoguns*, the Ashikaga family. |
| 1334 | Start of the Muromachi period—the Kenmu restoration; Emperor Go-Daigo attempts to take control of the country with the help of Ashikaga Takauji. |
| 1336 | Kyoto is captured by Ashikaga Takauji who takes military control of the country and forces Go-Daigo to move the southern court to Yoshino. |
| 1336–1574 | Ashikaga *bakufu*. Kyoto is reinstated as the capital. |
| 1338 | Takauji proclaims himself shogun and declares the northern court. |
| 1392 | The empire is unified when *shogun* |

**Right:** This seventeenth or eighteenth century print shows so-called "page boys" with their distinctive haircuts and red *hitatare* cloaks, keeping an eye on movements in the capital for the Taira. *British Museum/Jo St Mart*

**Below:** Two different types of quiver: the triple hollyhock mon below denotes the Tokugawa family.

| | Ashikaga Yoshimitsu receives the surrender of the southern court. |
|---|---|
| 1467–77 | The Onin War (civil war) witnesses the decline of the shogun's power and presaged the Sengoku *jidai* (The Age of Warring States) which lasts 150 years. Japan becomes split between rival *daimyos*. |
| 1542–3 | The first use of firearms in Japan as a shipwrecked Portuguese vessel at Tanegashima introduces the *harquebus*. |
| 1549 | (St.) Francis Xavier arrives in Japan. |
| 1560 | Oda Nobunaga begins the process of unifying Japan. Toyotomi Hideyoshi continues the quest after Nobunaga's death. |
| 1568–1603 | Azuchi-Momoyama period—civil war between samurai lords Tokugawa Ieyasu, Oda Nobunaga, and Toyotomi Hideyoshi as they battle for supremacy. |
| 1573 | Nobunaga overthrows the Muromachi *bakufu* giving him dominion over most of Japan. |
| 1575 | Battle of Nagashino—Nobunaga defeats the Takeda clan. |
| 1582 | Nobunaga assasinated by Akechi Mitsuhide and succeeded by Toyotomi Hideyoshi. |
| 1586 | Osaka castle built by Toyotomi Hideyoshi. |
| 1590 | Hideyoshi shogunate. |
| 1591 | Jesuits set up the first printing press in Japan. |
| 1592 | Hideyoshi invades Korea as part of a wider plan to invade China. |
| 1598 | Hideyoshi dies and Japanese troops withdrawal from Korea |
| 1600 | Battle of Sekigahara, Tokugawa Ieyasu defeats all contenders to become *shogun*. |

| | |
|---|---|
| 1600–1868 | Tokugawa Shogunate (Edo Period). This shogunate divides Japanese society into five hereditary classes—lords, samurai, farmers, artisans, and merchants. |
| 1614 | The Toyotomi clan is destroyed when Ieyasu captures Osaka castle. Christianity is banned from Japan. |
| 1615 | Tokugawa Ieyasu draws up the *Buke Sho Hatto* (Rules for Martial Families) before his death. It gave Samurai thirteen guides to living as a warrior during peacetime. |
| 1633 | Japan cuts ties with the outside world: *Shogun* Iemitsu bans foreign travel and foreign books, then later also forbids shipbuilding. |
| 1637–38 | Shimabara uprising of Christians. |
| 1641 | All foreigners except Dutch and Chinese are banned from Japan by Iemitsu. |
| 1650 | *Bushido* (way of the warrior) marks the growth of a new kind of samurai as a literate and virtuous warrior. |
| 1688–1704 | Genroku era; flowering of merchant culture. |
| 1701 | The Ako incident: Lord Asano attacks Lord Kira and is forced to commit *seppuku*. |
| 1703 | 47 *ronin* attack the mansion of Kira, and kill him; they are later ordered to commit *seppuku* |
| 1707 | Major eruption of Mt Fuji lasting sixteen days. |
| 1716 | Kyoho reforms intiated by Yoshimune, eighth *shogun*. |
| 1854 | Japan reopens to the outside world as the U.S. insists on the Treaty of Kanagawa trade agreement. |
| 1867 | 15th Tokugawa *Shogun* Tokugawa Yoshinobu resigns allowing the restoration of imperial rule. |
| 1868 | January—Emperor Mutsuhito officially |

regains his traditional powers and takes the name Meiji and is attributed with divine powers. The capital is established in Edo (Tokyo).

Boshin War starts between forces of the Tokugawa shogunate and the Satsuma and Choshu clans.

January 27, Battle of Toba-Fushimi sees defeat of Tokugawa shogunate forces.

| | |
|---|---|
| 1869 | The emperor takes return of the *daimyo* lands. |
| 1870 | Private armies are forbidden and the feudal system is dismantled. |
| 1873 | Meiji establishes an army based on conscription. Japan adopts the Gregorian calendar and grants universal religious freedom of conscience. |
| 1876 | Emperor Meiji declares a new law banning the wearing of swords in public. With this act the samurai ceased to be regarded as a separate social class after almost 1,000 years. |
| 1877 | Satsuma Rebellion. The last gasp of the samurai as dissaffected ex-samurai revolt against the emperor and his restrictions. Campaign ends at battle of Shiroyama where charismatic leader Saiga Takamori dies. |

**Left:** This nineteenth century photograph shows a group of samurai in traditional armor—although by the 1860s and 1870s they had espoused European fighting techniques. Note the enormous tetsubo—war club— at left. *via Clive Sinclaire*

189

# Bibliography

I am indebted to F.W Seal and C.E West for the considerable body of research done for the excellent Samurai Archives website. The major textual sources are detailed below. Note that some were sourced through the British Library article retrieval service and others through JSTOR, and Questia, the online reference library.

Berg, Richard H.: "Shogun Triumphant," *Command Magazine*, Jul–Aug. 1993, pp14–27.

Bottomley, I. and Hopson, A.P.: *Arms and Armor of the Samurai*; Bison Books, London.

Bryant, Anthony J.: *Samurai 1550-1600*; Osprey Publishing, Oxford. 1994.

*The Samurai;* Osprey Publishing, Oxford. 1989.

*Sekigahara*; Osprey Publishing, Oxford. 1995.

Collcutt, M.: "The 'Emergence of the Samurai' and the military history of early Japan," *Harvard Journal of Asiatic Studies*, 56: pp151–164, 1996.

Conlan, T. D.: "The nature of warfare in fourteenth-century Japan: the Record of Nomoto Tomoyuki," *Journal of Japanese Studies* 25: pp299–330, 1999.

Davis, D. L.: "The evolution of bushido to the year 1500." *JOSA* 13: pp38–56, 1978.

Farris, W. W.: *Heavenly warriors: the evolution of Japan's military; 500–1300*; Cambridge, Mass.: Council of East Asian Studies, Harvard University, 1992.

Friday, K.: "Teeth and claws: provincial warriors and the Heian court,"*Monumenta Nipponica* 43: pp153–185, 1988.

*Hired swords: the rise of private warrior power in early Japan.* Stanford University Press, 1992.

"Pushing beyond the pale: the Yamato conquest of the Emishi and Northern Japan," *Journal of Japanese Studies* 23: pp1–24, 1997

"Valorous butchers: the art of war during the golden age of the samurai," *Japan Forum* 5 (1): pp1–19, 1993.

*Samurai, warfare and the state in early medieval Japan*; Routledge, 2004, London.

Friday, K. F. & Seki,F.: *Legacies of the Sword: The Kashima-Shinryu and Samurai Martial Culture*; Hawai'i UP, 1997, Honolulu.

Gay, S.: "The Kawashima: warrior peasants of medieval Japan," *Harvard Journal of Asiatic Studies*, 46: pp81–119, 1986.

Gabriel, Richard A. and Boose, Donald W. Jr.: *The Great battles of Antiquity: A strategic and tactical guide to the great battles that shaped the development of war*; Westport. Greenwood Press, CT. 1994.

Griess, Thomas E., ed.: *The Dawn of Modern Warfare.* : Avery Publishing Group, New Jersey. 1984.

McCullough, Helen Craig (translator and editor).: *The Taiheiki*; Tuttle, New York. 1956.

Nobuyuki, Tamaru, ed.:*Strategy, Tactics, Weapons: Japanese Age of Battles edition*; Gakken, Tokyo, 1994.

Rabinovitch, Judith N. (translator).: *Shomonki: The Story of Masakado's Rebellion*; Sophia University Press, Tokyo, 1968.

Sansom, George: *A History of Japan to 1334*; Stanford University Press,Stanford, California. 1958.

Shinoda, Minoru: *The Founding of the Kamakura Shogunate 1180-1185*; Columbia University Press, New York. 1960.

Solum, Terje and Rue, Anders K.: *Saga of the samurai—Takeda rises to power*; Brookhurst Press, Anaheim. 2003.

*Saga of the samurai—Takeda Nobutora—the Unification of Kai*; Brookhurst Press, Anaheim. 2004.

*Saga of the samurai—Takeda Shingen*; Brookhurst Press, Anaheim. 2005.

*Saga of the samurai—Shingen in Command*; Brookhurst Press, Anaheim. 2006.

Takeuchi, R.: *The rise of the warriors*; CHJ 2, 1999.

Turnbull, Stephen R.: *Samurai Armies 1550-1615*; Osprey Publishing, London. 1979.

*Samurai Commanders 1577-1638*; Osprey Publishing, 2002.

*The Book of the Samurai*; Gallery Books, New York. 1982.
*Samurai Warriors*; Blandford Press, London. 1987.
*Battles of the Samurai*; Arms and Armor Press, London. 1987.
*Samurai Warlords*; Blandford Press, London. 1989.
*The Samurai—A Military History*; Macmillan Publishing, New York. 1977.
*War in Japan 1467–1615*; Osprey Publishing, Oxford. 2002.
*Samurai Warfare*; Arms and Armor Press, London. 1996.

*Genghis Khan & the Mongol Conquests, 1190–1400*; Routledge, New York. 2003.
Varley, Paul: *Warriors of Japan, as portrayed in the War tales*; University of Hawaii Press. 1994.
Wilson, William R.: *Hogen monogatari—Tale of the disorder of Hogen*; Cornell, 2001.
Yoshikawa Eiji (translated by Fuki Wooyenaka Uramatsu): *The Heike Story*; Tuttle, Vermont. 1956.
Zöllner, R.: "The profane wars of the heavenly warriors: reassessing medieval warfare," *Monumenta Nipponica* 61: pp219–226, 2006.

# Index